Astrological Signatures

– Course 2 –

Astrological
Signatures

Evolution of the Soul and the
Nature of Astrological Energies

C. C. Zain

The Church of Light
111 S. Kraemer Blvd., Suite A
Brea, CA 92821

800 500 0453
FAX: 714 255 9121
www.light.org

The Church of Light
111 S. Kraemer Blvd., Suite A
Brea, CA 92821

.6

Individual chapters originally copyrighted in 1926–1928 by
Elbert Benjamine.

Library of Congress Cataloging-in-Publication Data
Zain, C. C. (Elbert Benjamine), 1881–1951.
    Astrological signatures : evolution of the soul and the nature of
    astrological energies / C.C. Zain. —Rev. 2nd ed.
        p.   cm.   — (The Brotherhood of Light : course 2)
    Originally published: [S. 2.] : E. Benjamine, 1928.
    Includes index.
    ISBN 0-87887-372-4 (alk. paper) : $14.95
    1. Astrology. 2. Soul—Miscellanea. 3. Reincarnation—
Miscellanea. 4. Occultism I. Title. II. Series.
BF1711.Z35 1994   94-32270
133.5—dc20   CIP

Astrological Signatures may be obtained through your local bookstore
or you may order it from The Church of Light, 2341 Coral Street,
Los Angeles, CA 90031-2916, (213)226-0453.

(∞)   Printed on long-lasting acid-free paper.

Contents

List of Horoscopes _____

THE

2

Chapter 1

The Two Keys

I n all ages and in every land and clime there are progressive souls whose spiritual vision pierces the murky clouds of dogmatic illusion with which priestcraft and statecraft have ever sought to obscure the sun of divine truth. These bold aspirants to esoteric wisdom have the courage to burst the fetters that chain them to the lifeless creeds which are forced upon a benighted world. They free themselves from the thraldom of prejudice, and from that of servility to popular opinion. They intrepidly turn their faces from the blackness of the dead ages to knock resolutely at the door of the Temple of Knowledge. They realize that only within the sacred precincts of nature's sanctuary burn the altar fires whose light produces the shadowy illusions which are believed by the multitudes who worship them to be the only reality. And they learn that this sanctuary may be unlocked only by the use of two keys.

Such a candidate for initiation, having become as a little child, after divesting himself alike of the shroud of orthodoxy and the incumbrance of current scientific opinion—the one as dogmatic as the other—stands at the entrance of the temple, seeking admittance. This structure is the edifice of nature, the home of Isis, the lodge room of our Grand Master, King Sol; and is referred to in the Bible as Solomon's Temple. Now this name can hardly have been derived directly from so many divergent sources, yet in spite of this, SOL-OM-ON presents some interesting correspondences; for Sol is the Latin name of the Sun God Phoebus; Om is a Hindu name of Deity; and On is the Sun God of Heliopolis, Egypt, which anciently was called the City of On.

The candidate has heard it said, "Knock and it will open; Ask and ye shall receive; Seek and ye shall find." So, sustained by a love of justice, he stands with clean hands and a pure heart at the gate to

1

the sanctuary. After a time his efforts are rewarded by glimpses of the interior as the gates are opened by other hands, or the intuitions of his soul penetrate their opaqueness. His summons are finally answered by the Voice of the Silence, encouraging him to further endeavor; but at the same time admonishing him that there is no vicarious atonement or attainment. Each must unlock the doors that bar his progress and that guard the temple from profanation, for himself.

King Solomon's Temple has two doors; so also, there are two doors to its oracle. He who would enter either must possess their respective keys. The door on the right is opened only with the aid of a golden key; that on the left requires a key of silver. These same two keys with which the outer doors of the temple may be unlocked will also open the doors of the oracle; but the keys that are turned from right to left in the outer doors must be turned from left to right to unlock the inner.

That keys are extant by which their possessor may penetrate the barriers of objective phenomena is common knowledge among all well posted occultists. Students of masonic symbolism go further; for they recognize that these keys are two in number.

In fact, the literature on ceremonial magic very largely revolves around the two productions, the one entitled, "Clavicula Solomonis" (The Key of Solomon the King), and the other entitled, "Lemegeton" (Lesser Key), there being an English translation of both. But the usefulness of these volumes, if they may be said to have a use, pertains to the history of mystical aberration, and to magical practices of doubtful quality, rather than to any revelation of the mysteries.

Turning from these again to freemasonry, we find the symbol associated with the Fellow Craft degree to be complex. We are in search of keys, therefore the other symbology need not here concern us. But one prominent feature of the symbol are Two Crossed Keys, one of Silver and the other of Gold. These are the keys for which we seek. Masonry in its symbolism has preserved the keys to initiation. They are the keys that unlock the doors of King Solomon's Temple; but precisely what these two keys symbolize in occult science no modern expounder, in so far as I have been able to learn, has explained. Therefore, I shall devote this lesson to bringing to the notice of all and sundry who are interested in occult matters, both the importance and the nature of the key of silver and the key of gold.

The better to understand the conditions which confront the

present day searcher after truth, let us review the past with an eye to discerning the method by which whatever of enlightenment we now possess was gained. Perchance that method will give us a clue to the manner in which the many perplexities that now confront us may be solved.

Turning back the pages in the book of history a few hundred years, we find the utmost confusion in the realm of scientific thought. Prior to the seventeenth century material science was a wild jumble of notions. It was as great a medley of inconsistencies as we find today in the realm of religion and mysticism. And even as today assertions regarding religion are thought to be proved by citing authorities, so then the facts of material science rested upon authority as their final criterion. Just as mystics and religionists now feel free to give the particular interpretation of an authority—the Bible, for instance—that best suits their convenience, so then students were equally free in giving their own interpretation of scientific authorities. The controversies and animosities of present day religious sects and mystic cults are paralleled by the contention and turmoil in scientific circles preceding the seventeenth century.

This conflict between various schools was at an acute stage when, early in the seventeenth century, an event occurred which revolutionized the methods of scientific thought. The existing chaos of science was well recognized. Therefore, in the hope of establishing some kind of order, Cardinal Bagne called together the notables and savants of his time to listen to the discourse of a scholar, M. Chandoux, who expounded the principles of a new philosophy. Present at that discourse was young René Descartes.

M. Chandoux was an eloquent speaker and clothed his thoughts in flowery language. With one exception his hearers were convinced and applauded loudly. The exception was René Descartes.

An acquaintance, noticing Descartes' reticence, asked him to explain in what manner he disapproved of the new principles so eloquently presented. Descartes complimented the speaker highly upon his ability, and then voiced an axiom that every occult student should constantly bear in mind. It is due to the failure to realize the importance of this fact that a thousand and one intellectual crudities are being palmed off on a credulous world today. He said: "Nothing Can Be Proved or Disproved by Unproved Principles."

What was true of material science in Descartes' time is equally true in regard to occultism, mysticism, and religion at present: "The probable being often substituted for the true, it being easy to mistake the fictitious for the true when dressed in false guise."

To illustrate this, Descartes asked the assembly to give him some well recognized fact. Then, by means of twelve statements he proved the fact to be true. After which, he took twelve other statements, and, to the consternation of all present, proceeded with equal ease, and in an apparently irrefutable manner, to prove its falsity.

The experiment was repeated again and again, to the great dismay of his audience. A confusion resulted that resembles that of religion and occultism today. The apparently proven facts of man's proper relation to other entities in the universe and to Deity are subject to just such jugglery, to affirmation by some authorities and to denial by others; both being sustained by arguments. No wonder the student often doubts the possibility of knowing without mistake the real truth concerning anything.

So it was with Descartes' hearers. They began to doubt their ability ever to recognize the truth. Consequently they sought his opinion about the matter. His reply is quite as important to religion and occult science today as it then was to material science, and if his advice is followed it will work as important a change for their betterment as it then worked for the advancement of material knowledge. He stated that Mathematics Alone avoids sophisms, and by its aid All Problems can be Solved, if Proper Principles be Followed.

That was the beginning of what is now called exact science. Its success during the intervening years has been due to the ability of its votaries to follow proper mathematical principles. Furthermore, the incongruities of certain materialistic philosophers and scientists are due to their departure from mathematical methods and their attempting to prove their doctrines by unproved principles.

Now it is not my purpose to convey the idea that the physical intellect alone is capable of successfully wrestling with nature's arcane truths; for the soul, when free from the bondage of the physical senses, becomes a far superior judge of reality. The perceptions of the astral brain have a far greater range than those of the physical, and the sense organs of the spiritual body have even a much greater range than these. Furthermore, on the inner planes, intelligences of vastly greater ability than any on earth may be contacted. The soul when free from the body and functioning in a finer form is infinitely more capable of grasping the true inner significance of nature's wondrous manifestations.

But it is only the exceptional individual, under exceptional circumstances, who is able so to free himself from the limitations imposed by the flesh, that upon his soul's return to its earthy tenement from sublime flights in the starry realms of aeth his physical organism grasps the truths he has contacted without coloring them to conform to preconceived ideas, to prevalent opinions, or to the personal peculiarities due to centers of energy within his astral form that are mapped by his birth chart. The soul's experience may be compared to the pure white radiance of our sun, which is stained to different hues as it passes through colored cathedral windows.

People in general are greatly influenced by thought currents. Some dominant character puts forth an idea. Other less positive minds receive this idea either through unconscious thought transference, or through the written or spoken word. The positiveness with which the idea is launched enables it to gain a controlling power over a few. These then, having become dominated by the idea, formulate it anew. Thinking about it strongly, they send out astral waves that reach the astral brains of a whole nation. One after another people begin to accept the idea, and the more people there are thinking it the stronger becomes its power to dominate others.

The ease with which a few men in high political office often are able to warp the judgment of a whole people well illustrates this. No matter how pernicious or illogical the idea is, if it is launched strongly enough and gains momentum, it will dominate the majority. History abounds with the follies of whole nations temporarily so dominated. They are so under the power of suggestion that they fail to see the matter in any light but that under which it has been presented to them. They lose the power to reason about this particular thing, just as a hypnotized subject must accept what the operator suggests without question, and may imagine he is quite logical and rational. Likewise, the memory of the soul's experiences when free from the physical body has a tendency to be warped by thought currents into conformity with them.

There is also a tendency, deeply rooted in the makeup of the astral body, on the part of mystical minds to be controlled by autosuggestion. They sometimes become so dominated by some religious belief, or by some phantasy that has gained a strong hold in the astral brain, that the meaning of both physical and astral experiences is greatly distorted to confirm it. If there is much egotism, conversation with any disembodied entity may be construed as talking directly with Deity, even though others recognize the entity as an elemental. In such cases the mystic follows the dictates of the voice, even if it leads to death. And even where no such dominant idea is present, early beliefs often are so strongly entrenched in the astral brain as to considerably color the memory of experiences brought back from excursions into higher realms. Consequently, there is always the need of critical analysis of such experiences, and the application of as competent methods as possible to test their accuracy. Such methods are embraced within the silver and golden keys.

Let us consider that nature in all her various manifestations is under law, and that this law invariably is based upon mathematical principles. Mathematical relations are absolute, and pertain as well to spiritual, celestial and angelic spheres, as they do to our humble planet. Everything, from the tremor of a thought wave to the evolution of a universe, operates in strict obedience to numerical law. The eight volved tower of Babel rose on Shinar's plain to exemplify the numbers understood by the Magi to govern race evolution. The pyramids yet stand as a monumental proof of the numerical relations existing between the earth, the universe, and the soul of man. And though the Pythagorean system of numbers was never placed in writing, and hence is dimly grasped except by the few, yet its fame has echoed down the corridors of time and prompts our soul to listen to the music of the spheres.

Mathematics alone enables one to avoid mental pitfalls, and it is due to this fact that the Golden and Silver keys are the most valuable possessions that the occultist can obtain in the world of mental research; for they are each grounded in, and strictly built upon numerical proportions.

To comprehend their function we must have recourse to the Written and Oral Laws.

Initiates understand the Written Law to be that Law inscribed in scintillating characters of light, by the ever moving finger of Deity, in the azure dome that spans our midnight sky. It is written in the Language of the Stars, and thus revealed His will to the primitive Assyrian Shepherds. Its study later gave to Egypt her splendor, and made the Chaldean Magi so justly famous. It was the knowledge of this ineffaceable Written Law, the sublime science of the starry heavens, that constituted the wisdom that flowed from the magical schools of Atlantis toward the rising sun; and in the dim and distant past, in those remoter periods of racial childhood, before material struggles had crystallized the sensitiveness of the soul, it was the pure intuitional recognition of the Written Law that constituted primitive religion.

Man is an epitome of the universe; is, in fact, a universe in miniature, built upon the exact plan and proportions of the larger one. His component parts interact with one another, even as do the orbs of nature; and they also interact with those larger bodies. Man, in his ignorance, imagines himself an isolated unit; but as his vision expands, he more and more recognizes the unity existing between himself and his divine source; and between himself and the infinitude of other manifestations.

Can we wonder then, realizing the mystical relation that exists between the soul and the stars, that a primitive people whose spiritual faculties were infinitely more sensitive and active than our own, should formulate their system of religion to conform to the heavenly bodies? They worshipped Deity by striving to learn and obey His laws. The Heavenly Father was looked upon as a benefic being whose mandates were to be obeyed, even as a child places loving confidence in the wisdom of its parents.

Observation had convinced these primitive races that everything of importance occurred conformably to the position and movements of the heavenly bodies. The recurrence of certain celestial phenomena always brought the rains of winter; other positions ever heralded the time for sowing, and the time for harvest. The rivers overflowed their banks when at dusk or dawn certain stars were in the ascendant; and the tides of human life, as well as those of the sea, ebbed and flowed in obedience to the dictates of the heavenly orbs. These children of nature worshipped Deity by obedience to the dictates of nature. And it was only because they had become convinced that it is God's method of instructing His children that they bowed in reverence to the Written Law.

Thus it need not surprise us to find the remnants of an Astronomical Religion in every land. Being founded upon long ages of carefully tabulated facts, as well as subject to searching verification by specially qualified souls, it constituted a Science as well as a Religion. The qualities and interior principles of stellar influence were made the subject of systematic study for centuries; and their correspondences were located, both on the earth and in the human constitution. This religion was the worship of nature's laws.

In after years, when only a few could comprehend its scientific aspect because of spiritual and mental degeneration due to cyclic changes, the result of these studies was formulated into myths, each portraying the attributes and qualities of some stellar orb or celestial phenomenon. Certain qualities ascribed to Deity in his manifestations through the orbs and stars thus became the object of special worship by some people. Fire worship, sex worship, serpent worship, all sprang from this source; as well as the worship of mythological characters, who always portray with accuracy the qualities of celestial bodies. It certainly would greatly surprise the orthodox devotees of the twentieth century if they could but know how much of their religion is borrowed, with little or no alteration, from astronomical worship.

Astronomy is the Written Law; and the Golden Key to its interpretation is Astrology.

This golden key is constructed strictly upon mathematical lines; is, in fact, the only means of positively applying mathematics to the door of the past and future, and thus minimizing the chance of error. The student ignorant of its use can never realize the relation of his soul to the universe; nor comprehend astromasonry, astrotheology, nor astromythology. The philosophy and religion of the ancients will be to him a perplexing labyrinth; because they are founded upon the principles of astronomy and astrology. It is by the use of this key alone that natural sympathies and antipathies become understandable; and the cyclic locks that alike are found to guard men, nations, worlds, and starry systems, are turned in their wards by the hand of the mind only by its aid.

This golden key unlocks the door of positive knowledge in King Solomon's Temple. It reveals the why and wherefore of man's past, present, and future condition. It is mathematical certainty alike in religion, philosophy, and science; for it deals not with effects, but with causes. The alchemist who neglects the golden key will seek in vain to transmute base metals into gold, and will fail utterly in producing the elixir vitae. The physician ignorant of its use, be he homeopathic, allopathic, chiropractic, osteopathic, mental scientist, christian scientist, or divine healer, will in many instances receive unexpected results from his best efforts; because he fails to grasp the inner magnetic relation of his patient, himself, and the method he employs. What is one man's poison is another's cure; and this may be magnetic poison, or mental, as well as physical; and these inner sympathies and antipathies only become recognized through familiarity with the principles of astrology.

It is a generally accepted fact that nations rise and fall with rhythmic precision; but such periods of ascension and decline can only be known by use of the golden key. Our government may continue to endow meteorological stations with millions, but the state of the weather will never be known more than a few days in advance until they recognize this key; and man without its proper use will continue to grope in darkness where spiritual facts are concerned.

The golden key alone made possible the wonderful cures wrought by Paracelsus, it guided the mystic Jacob Boehme in the erection of a religious and philosophical system; and in all past ages it has constituted the most reliable chart for those souls who boldly attempted to sail the wide ocean of spiritual research. It has been the means by which, at last, they have reached the haven of attainment.

But now let us again consider more primitive times. The intellectual and spiritual condition of the world is, like all things manifest, subject to cyclic law; and there have been recurring periods of comparative light and comparative darkness. After the mental forces have spent themselves in any age, they begin to wane, and the race declines into barbaric ignorance. When these periodic conditions of spiritual decline set in, there is an effort made upon the part of the most enlightened to preserve their knowledge for the few who will be able to appreciate it during the dark ages to follow, those who will pass it on in substance to future generations when the spiritual forces again rise in the world's ascendant. Thus originated the Hermetic Schools which are custodians of the Secret Doctrine.

The hierophants of these schools collect as many facts as possible relating to spiritual things, and formulate them into allegorical systems suitable for communication by word of mouth. In order that these mysteries shall not become entirely lost they are frequently given, in part or as a whole, to the populace. Such allegories become the religious doctrine of the multitude, and passing into writing may constitute a holy book. Thus originated the Vedas, the Avesta, the Bible, and other sacred writings. But as a rule, at their inception, these traditions have been transmitted orally, by word of mouth, and thus are known to initiates as "The Oral Law."

The Oral Law is the Secret Doctrine, and having been formulated by the Magi, it is constructed in such a manner as to be incomprehensible to the vulgar, yet not difficult of interpretation to one possessing its key. This key was explained only during the course of initiation into the mysteries, after the recipient had proven indisputably his physical, intellectual, and moral integrity. And just here it may be well to digress long enough to explain that, following in the literary custom, I use the masculine pronoun in these lessons to include both sexes; for never has woman been barred from membership and equal privileges with her brothers in any true Hermetic School. The doors of Luxor, Rosicrucia, and The Brotherhood of Light, have ever welcomed her.

But to proceed: This open sesame to all traditional knowledge exists at the present day and has been recognized and used advantageously by a number of eminent kabalists, mystics, and savants; but has received scant attention from those outside the portals of certain secret societies. This Silver Key to the Oral Law is none other than the Sacred Tarot, or Book of Thoth. From its pages the illuminated St. Martin drew inspiration. Aided by, and in strict conformity to its revelations, the savant, Eliphas Levi, wrote his truly marvelous work, *The Dogma and Ritual of Transcendental Magic*. This key was held in the highest esteem by the erudite Count de Gebelin; was the basis of William Postel's *Key of Things Kept Secret from the Foundation of the World*; and constituted the *Ars Magna* of Raymond Lully, by which he claimed all problems might be solved. Lully was a profound kabalist, and the crowning effort of his life was his philosophical wheel, or method of applying the Tarot.

Not only do archaeologists find remnants of the golden key in all portions of the world, but by their side fragments from the key of silver. The Book of Thoth, under various names, was known to remotest antiquity. It was formulated by the same master minds who peopled the starry heavens with mystic characters and forged the golden key to their interpretation, to serve as the handmaiden to religious astrology.

Now the golden key has a stem of twenty-two symbols—twelve zodiacal signs and ten planets. It has a ring of four decades—thirty-six decanates and four seasons of the sun's annual cycle. It has wards, consisting of the twelve mundane mansions and the elemental ruler of each of the four quadrants, that turn in three worlds. In its action it is masculine and positive.

The silver key is a duplicate of the one of gold, except that in its action it is feminine and passive, thus bearing the same relation to the latter that woman bears to man. The twenty-two Major Arcana of the Tarot each bear an exact correspondence to one of the twelve zodiacal signs or ten planets and constitute an esoteric interpretation of them. The forty numbered Minor Arcana bear a strict relation to the thirty-six decanates and the four seasons of the sun's annual cycle. The sixteen members of the Tarot Court accurately describe the twelve mundane mansions and the elemental ruler of each of the four quadrants.

In fact, the Tarot bears the same relation to astrology that the Moon bears to the Sun, and even as the Sun illuminates the day, so does astrology shed its radiance upon the more evident truths of occultism. But those deeper and more recondite mysteries remaining in the shadow cast by objective existence would forever remain in the dark, even as at night nothing is seen until the Moon has risen, were it not for the soft radiance of the silver key. It is true, the moon shines by borrowed light; yet we are grateful for her rays. Just so the Tarot borrows her significance from her heavenly spouse, astrology; yet she sheds an ever welcome illumination upon our darkest mental paths.

Bearing this explanation in mind a much quoted passage from the Zohar, one of the books of the Jewish Kabalah, becomes luminous. It runs thus: "At the death of Moses the sun was eclipsed and the Written Law lost its splendor, and at the death of David the moon diminished and the Oral Law was tarnished."

Moses according to tradition—and the word kabalah means traditions—was raised by the Egyptian Magi, and was initiated into the mysteries. Consequently he was familiar with both astronomy and the kabalah, or the Written Law and the Oral Law; and had been given the keys to their interpretation. In fact, the story of creation as allegorically given in Genesis, when correctly interpreted, is capable of a mathematical proof that harmonizes with the law of cycles as known to present day initiates. Furthermore, the whole Pentateuch, by whomsoever written, teems with thinly veiled references to astronomical cycles, laws, qualities, and movements. As these references are found to coincide with observed phenomena, they indicate a deep knowledge of astrology, the golden key, upon the part of their composer. So the kabalists, having reference to the positive illuminating power of the golden key, compared it to the sun. This sun, meaning astrology, was eclipsed at the death of Moses. Its proper use was lost to the Jews; hence the Written Law, astronomy, lost its splendor, or became meaningless. And this fact is confirmed by Bible study.

The silver key, the intuitional, feminine counterpart of astrology, was compared to the moon, which diminished at the death of David. That is, the Jews were skilled in the meaning and use of the Tarot down to the time of David, but at his death they lost the final key to their mysteries, hence the Oral Law was tarnished. They yet retained the Bible and the kabalah, but had lost the key to their interpretation; and when a part of the latter finally was committed to writing, the ignorance of this key on the part of its scribes gave to it a garbled form.

The ark of the covenant, which the Children of Israel ever carried with them was a synthetic representation of the Tarot, or Book of Thoth. Now the silver key has wards opening the three worlds of existence. Corresponding to these are the three stories of the ark. The base was of square form to represent the physical world and the alchemical kingdom of salt. Each of the two rings on either side, through which were thrust the carrying poles, thus represents the number ten, the sacred emanations of the Sephiroth. The four rings collectively represent the Sephiroth in all four of the elemental realms, corresponding in this to the forty Minor Arcana of the Tarot. As mind is superior to matter, the coffer just above the base corresponds to the intellectual world and the alchemical kingdom of mercury. This is represented in the Tarot by the human figures that constitute the Court Arcana. The divine world was symbolized by the uppermost section, that region above the mercy seat. This corresponds alchemically to the kingdom of sulphur, and in the Tarot is represented by the twenty-two Major Arcana, typifying as they do the signs and planets of heaven whose influence is ever active upon both the lower forms of life and the actions of men.

In this ark were carried[1] the four symbolical suits of the Tarot. There was the golden pot, or suit of cups. Aaron's rod that budded represents the suit of scepters. The tables of the covenant, or law, correspond to the suit of swords; and the mana contained in the golden pot well symbolizes the suit of coins.

The cherubs at either end of the mercy seat typify in the divine world the Father-Motherhood of God, in the intellectual world the rational and intuitional methods of gaining knowledge, and in the physical world the positive and negative forces of nature. Kabalists assert that it was between the wings of these cherubs that the high priests consulted the Lord by means of Teraphim, Urim, Thummim, and by Ephod; and such biblical mention as is made of the matter tends to confirm the opinion. This method was none other than the use of the silver key, the sacred Tarot.

This is but one of the many examples that might be cited to show an early knowledge of the silver key upon the part of the Hebrews; but their later writings, with some exceptions, do not indicate the same familiarity with it. Ezekiel evidently recovered it, for by its application alone can the mystic symbology of his writings be intelligently interpreted. Daniel also evinces some knowledge of its use;

and the whole Apocalypse, whoever its author may have been, is based upon the Tarot. In fact, each of the twenty-two chapters is an exemplification of one of the twenty-two Major Arcana in its relation with the others, as applied to prophecy. Thus it well may be said that at the death of David it was lost to the Jewish priesthood, yet it is equally certain that afterwards it was recovered by some of the inspired prophets.

Not only the Bible but the sacred writings of other nations of antiquity may be interpreted by use of the silver key; for their allegories came alike from a common source, and have suffered minor alterations due to later environment. We may confidently say, then, that no one can thoroughly understand the inner meaning of the ancient sacred books who is ignorant of the Tarot. Or, stating it in the words of Eliphas Levi we may say:

> Without the Tarot, the magic of the ancients is a closed book, and it is impossible to penetrate any of the great mysteries of the Kabalah.

We may be sure that the gigantic intellects who first discovered the Written Law, and who formulated the Oral Law, perceived in nature a unity whose ever varying manifestations are due to certain fundamental principles. The universe is but the action and reaction of these principles under the dominion of one law, and this law conforms strictly to mathematical relations. These mathematical relations once discovered through observation of the Written Law, it was but a step to incorporate them in the Oral Law. Likewise they are maintained in, and contribute to the value of, the silver key.

The keen intuitions and spiritual perceptions of the ancient Magi enabled them to formulate the exact correspondence between the soul and the stars. They likewise forged the golden key as a means of unlocking this realm of positive knowledge. But the inner, more secret, intuitive interpretations; wherein they often exemplified the personal experience of the soul in other realms than this, required a key of different composition. Therefore, in its construction they employed the language of universal symbolism. The silver key, constructed as a mathematical duplicate of its golden counterpart, if intelligently applied, will not fail to open one of the principal doors to King Solomon's Temple.

In fact, the traditions of freemasonry aver that owing to the death of one of their grand masters the master mason's word was lost, and with it the key to certain of their mysteries. At a later date, through an accidental discovery, the lost word and lost key were recovered. This discovery is represented as the disinterment of the ark of the covenant containing the four emblems that each mark one suit of the Tarot.

From the ark are taken, first the Book of Laws, and then four pieces of paper or scrolls of parchment bearing the key to the characters of their mysteries. As has been mentioned, the ark of the covenant is a symbolical synthesis of the Tarot. The Book of Laws represents the Oral Law. The four scrolls of parchment signify the four quadrants of the heavens upon which is inscribed the characters of the Written Law.

The master's word is found upon the ark, covered with three squares, which are the jewels of the three ancient grand masters. These jewels are astronomical measures, and form a portion of the golden key.

Freemasonry undoubtedly is derived from the ancient mysteries of initiation. Each of the first thirty-two degrees is founded upon one of the ten numbered Arcana, or one of the twenty-two Major Arcana. The members of the lodge by whom the candidate is surrounded are represented by the Court Arcana. The thirty-third degree is typified in the Tarot by the mystic seal. These degrees also correspond to the thirty-three chapters of the kabalistical book, Sephir Yetzirah, or Book of Formation, which, founded upon the Tarot, has thirty-three chapters, and is explained by a commentary entitled, "The Thirty-two Paths of Wisdom." As masonic ritual is based upon the Tarot, its esoteric meaning is only comprehensible when proper application is made of the silver key.

Nor is the use of the silver key confined to revealing the mysteries of antiquity, for it can advantageously be applied to the solution of all the problems of science and philosophy.

> Letters are absolute ideas; absolute ideas are numbers; numbers are perfect signs. In reuniting ideas to numbers we can operate upon ideas as upon numbers and arrive at the mathematics of truth.[2]
> Thus the possibilities of the Tarot are only limited by the ability of its user. Its prevalent abuse as a divinatory instrument, it is true, has brought it somewhat into disrepute. Yet while not denying the effectiveness of either the golden key or the silver key in divination, I should not fail to emphasize that this is the lowest plane of their usefulness, and that their application to spiritual matters will yield the seeker far superior rewards for effort expended.

Again to quote Levi in regard to the Tarot:

> It is a truly philosophical machine, which keeps the mind from
> going astray while leaving its initiative and liberty; it is mathe-
> matics applied to the absolute, the alliance of the positive and the
> ideal, a lottery of thought as exact as numbers, perhaps the simplest
> and grandest conception of human genius.

This is a stupendous thought. And lest the reader be given the
impression that there is something complex and difficult in the
principle underlying the golden key and the silver key, before bringing this lesson to a close, I shall risk introducing an element of
crudeness by descending from philosophical concepts to the most
material and commonplace matters of which, at the moment, I can
think.

For the sake of illustration only, and admitting it to be rather an
undignified example, let us suppose that a man desired to build and
furnish a dwelling.

He is confronted with purchasing quite an assortment of things,
and it becomes necessary to know how much of each to purchase,
and what the cost will be. He must have dimension lumber, siding,
sheeting, brick, nails, sand, lime, plumbing fixtures, and many other
things in addition to paying for the labor. How is he to determine
the influence of this proposed dwelling upon his bank account?

Obviously, he can not merely visualize the house as built and
furnished, and from such a picture draw any accurate conclusions
as to its complete cost. Nor will visualizing the materials as brought
together in crude piles assist him much.

Now lumber is sold by the board foot. Therefore, having recourse
to mathematics, he determines how many board feet of each kind of
lumber are required. Then, multiplying each kind by the price per
foot for that kind, and adding together the various prices so obtained
he arrives at the cost of his lumber bill.

But brick, being sold by the thousand, cannot be computed in
board feet. To find the cost of the brick required he must multiply
the number of thousand brick by the cost per thousand.

Sand is sold neither by the thousand nor by the board foot, but
by the yard. The number of yards of sand required multiplied by the
price per yard, therefore, gives him the cost of the sand.

Nails, which are also required, are not sold by the thousand, nor
by the yard, nor by the board foot, but by the pound. Consequently,
to find the cost of the nails he must multiply the number of pounds

of nails by the price per pound.

Without going into the details of other requirements; such as lime, sold by the barrel; wall paper, sold by the roll; rugs, sold by the square foot; chinaware, sold by the dozen; and skilled labor, sold by the hour; it is quite evident that an accurate estimate of each requirement can only be made by first associating it with its own symbol of commensuration. Nails cannot be computed by associating them with board feet, but they can be computed by associating them, according to proper mathematical principles, with pounds, which is their proper symbol of commensuration. Furthermore, when each requirement has been properly associated with its own symbol of commensuration, and through this its cost calculated, by then adding together the prices of these various items the cost of the completed dwelling may be made known.

So much for boards, and nails, and chinaware, and the even more familiar commodity, human labor.

But even as there is a symbol of commensuration for each of these common things, by which alone its influence upon the bank account may be ascertained, so likewise is there a symbol of commensuration for every object and force in the universe, by which alone its true quality and influence may be made known. These are astrological terms. As has been shown in an earlier lesson, everything, in its vibratory rate, corresponds to some astrological quality. Even ideas and spiritual principles have astrological correspondences. Therefore, by associating the symbol of its astrological correspondence with anything we are using its own symbol of commensuration; and much as board foot associated with lumber enables it to be measured, so the astrological term enables us to form a just estimate of other things.

Furthermore, when things are associated with their proper astrological symbols, and thus made commensurate, their influence upon each other or upon an individual may be learned. When stated in astrological terms the most diverse matters become commensurate. As nails and boards and sand and lime, when first made commensurate by associating each with its own proper symbol, and that stating in terms of dollars and cents, may thus be combined to give a total cost; so, by associating them first with their own astrological symbols, and then stating in terms of vibratory harmony and discord, the total influence upon human thought and life of the most diverse things may be known.

Among the most potent of these diverse things to influence the course of human life are invisible planetary rays. That we are unconscious of their power to influence us at certain times to think and act in one way, and at another time to think and act in an opposite manner, mitigates their influence not in the least. Is the sunflower, whose face follows the course of the sun, aware that its movements are influenced by light? Both plants and animals are continually influenced in their growth and behavior by gravitation, yet what is gravitation? Animals and plants, both in growth and in movement, respond markedly to changes in temperature. Subconsciously they may be aware of the desire that leads to these various behaviors, as no doubt man is subconsciously aware of the desire to act in a certain way because of his astral body being stimulated by planetary vibrations. Objectively he merely experiences certain impulses without knowing why. The moth does not know why it flies into the flame. It flies into it because light has the power of stimulating it to fly in the direction of the light. This tropism, as it is called, causes the moth to react to certain vibrations in a specific way, and another tropism causes man to react to planetary influence in a way that may not be dissimilar.

This, then, is the method incorporated into the two keys. They are constructed to reveal astrological correspondences and thus facilitate the use of the proper symbols of commensuration. They are constructed to indicate, once the proper symbols have been obtained, the influence of one thing or idea upon another. They include in their composition such mathematics as is necessary to determine the total harmony and discord, and hence the total influence, of the most diverse things when they are brought together. They constitute a means of measuring both special and universal forces.

In conclusion, I again state the words of Descartes, who, it may be mentioned, before settling down to his final life work, roamed the whole of Europe in search of someone who could initiate him into a secret occult fraternity; "Mathematics alone avoids sophisms."

In this we find the greatest commendation for the use of both the golden key and the silver key, for both conform to mathematical principles. And in no other field will the student be so well rewarded for his labor, and less likely to become grounded in error, than in applying to the macrocosm and the microcosm these two invaluable keys.

Notes

1. Hebrews 9.4.
2. *Dogmas and Ritual of Transcendental Magic*, by Eliphas Levi.

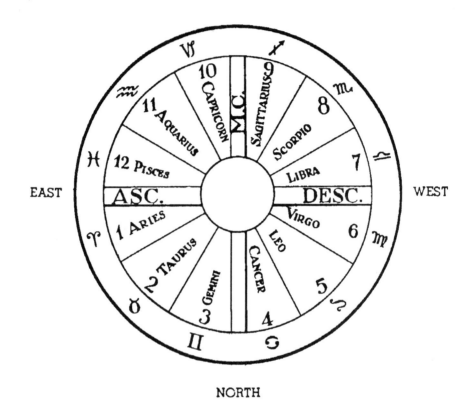

EAST   WEST

NORTH

SYMBOLS

♈ Aries   ♎ Libra
♉ Taurus   ♏ Scorpio
♊ Gemini   ♐ Sagittarius
♋ Cancer   ♑ Capricorn
♌ Leo   ♒ Aquarius
♍ Virgo   ♓ Pisces

Chapter 2 _____

The Zodiac

NY worth-while study of the occult sciences must be based upon familiarity with the golden key, Astrology. The various astral vibratory rates that constitute the occult properties of objects can only conveniently be classified by associating them in terminology with similar vibrations of the zodiacal signs and the planets. We have no other terminology than the astrological at present by which to designate the various astral forces, which are the chief subjects of study in the occult sciences. The language of the stars, then, is the only language we possess today by which we can converse intelligently of occult matters. The alphabet of this language has twenty-two letters comprising the ten planets and the twelve zodiacal signs. The planets constitute the vowels. In Chapter 3, Course 1, *Laws of Occultism,* I have already designated the chief vibratory quality of each planet. And now, that we may be familiar with the whole alphabet customarily used in occult discourse, I shall take up the discussion of the consonants, the Twelve Zodiacal Signs.

To begin with, we must understand of what the zodiac consists. The earth, in its annual journey around the sun, follows an elliptical path. This is the same path apparently followed by the sun. Because the eclipses of the sun and moon all take place along this path it is called the Ecliptic. In astrology, to avoid the constant repetition of the phrase, "sun, moon, and planets," it is customary to include all in the term "planets." The sun, strictly speaking, is not a planet but a star past middle age. Neither is the moon a planet. It is a satellite of the earth, relative to its own life processes hoary with years. With this definition in mind I may next say that none of the planets in their orbital revolutions move much to the north or south of the ecliptic. That is, none of them in its movement gets more than a few degrees away from the apparent path of the sun.

There is thus a belt arching the heavens from west to east from which the planets never wander. This belt was considered by the ancients, from whom much of our astrological knowledge is derived, to extend nine degrees north and nine degrees south of the apparent path of the sun. The very word "planet" means "wandering," and unlike the stars, the planets may be observed to meander along this path. The stars are self luminous suns, but the planets are masses of matter much smaller than our sun. They shine by reflected light, and held by the gravitational pull of the sun, revolve around it, as does the planet earth, in elliptical orbits. This belt, through which all the planets move, is mapped by starry constellations. These, for the most part, are traced to represent animals. Hence, as the word means "an animal," this belt through the sky, in the center of which is the apparent path of the sun, is called the Zodiac.

Bearing in mind that the center of the zodiac is the sun's path—for while it is really the earth that moves, yet to avoid countless repetition of the word "apparent" it is customary to speak as if it were the sun that moves—it is easy to see that the zodiac may have a definite starting point. The sun each year moves north from the southern celestial hemisphere to the northern celestial hemisphere, bringing with it the summer season. It does this because its path, the ecliptic, is inclined at an angle of 23 degrees, 26 minutes, 56 seconds to the plane of the earth's equator, the projection of which in the sky is called the Celestial Equator. Because the ecliptic and celestial equator are not identical and not parallel they must intersect each other. The line of their intersection is called the equinoctial colure. The points where the sun, following its path, the ecliptic, crosses the celestial equator, are called the vernal equinox and the autumnal equinox. They are called equinoxes because when the sun reaches these points the nights are equal in duration to the days.

Such terminology may seem slightly technical. Everyone, however, is familiar with the changes of the seasons from winter to spring and from summer to autumn. These changes are caused by the sun crossing the equinoctial colure, crossing from the southern celestial hemisphere to the northern celestial hemisphere about the 21st of March each year, and from the northern celestial hemisphere to the southern celestial hemisphere each year about the 23rd of September. These points in the path of the sun where it crosses the celestial equator are easily ascertained in the sky, and, since they usher in the two halves of the year, winter and summer, are manifestly of great importance.

Of these two points it is found experimentally that the one where the sun crosses the celestial equator in spring is the more important, and constitutes the commencement of the zodiac. The zodiac, then, though a circular belt in the sky, has a definite starting point. This starting point is not determined by any of the stars or constellations, but by the place among the stars and constellations during any given year where the sun crosses from south declination to north declination. It commences at the vernal, or spring, equinox.

There is undoubtedly a good reason, one that with sufficient knowledge could be traced, why man has ten fingers and ten toes, while a chicken has but four toes and only the atrophied remnants of fingers. We are accustomed to accept the number of toes an animal has without much questioning, merely because observation teaches us that it is common for certain creatures to possess a given number of digits. Likewise we may accept, because observation demonstrates it to be true, that there are twelve major divisions of the zodiac. Were we to delve deeply enough we undoubtedly should learn why twelve and not ten; but as observed in their influence upon human life there are twelve equal chief divisions. That is, starting at the point where the sun crosses the celestial equator in the spring, and following its path until again it crosses the celestial equator the following spring, some twelve months later, this circular pathway is found to have twelve equal segments, each segment possessing a vibratory influence peculiarly its own. Such a segment of the belt about the heavens, the center of which is the sun's path, is called a Sign of the Zodiac.

The signs of the zodiac should not be confused with the constellations. The position of the signs in the sky is referable to the position of the sun relative to the earth. The place among the stars where the sun crosses the celestial equator during the spring of any year is the point where the zodiac commences that year. This point constantly, but not uniformly, shifts in reference to the stars and constellations. It shifts back among the constellations—these being composed of stars—that lie along the zodiac at such a rate that it moves completely around the circle of stars in 25,868 years. This precessional movement is not uniform, but variable, almost ceasing at some times and at others becoming rapid. Thus while the average amount may be taken as 50.2" a year, should it be necessary to calculate the exact motion at any time, what is called the equation of the equinox must be taken into account, which is the difference between the actual position and the position had it moved uniformly. This backward movement of the commencing point of the zodiac is called the "precession of the equinoxes," and its motion through the constellations of stars gives rise to the various astrological ages.

So far as the effect is concerned it makes no difference whether the armature revolves around an electromagnet or the electromagnet revolves around the armature. The sun is an electromagnet, the lines of force from which are cut by the planets as they revolve around it. The stars of space also radiate energy, the lines of which are cut by the sun in its movement among them. Such fields of force as are radiated by our sun and by the stars probably vary in intensity in different places just as the field of force about a magnet varies at different points in a circle traced around it, due to the location of its poles. We need not be surprised, then, to find that the vibrations that reach the earth from the sun and planets from different sections of the circle they apparently make about the earth are dissimilar in quality and in power.

The celestial equator, coinciding on earth with the earth's equator, divides the earth astronomically into north and south polarity. And it is found experimentally that the relation of the sun to this division of the earth determines the relation of the earth to the various sections of the field of force through which the planets move. In other words, the signs of the zodiac owe their peculiar vibratory quality to the definite section of the heavens they occupy relative to the positions of the sun and earth. In determining these various intensities in the field of force through which the planets move, the stars seem to have little or no influence, for, although the zodiac shifts continually through the constellations, the influence of the signs of the zodiac throughout the ages has remained unchanged.

This is not the place to discourse of astrological Ages. But it would be amiss not to point out that the constellations do have an influence of their own, an influence that apparently is quite distinct from the signs although it must be gauged in association with them. I have already mentioned the backward shifting of the signs through the constellations. This apparent motion is caused by the attraction of the sun and moon on the earth's equator. The earth is flattened at the poles, being thicker at the equator. Hence the gravitational pull at the equator is greater, and as the equator is inclined to the plane of pull of the sun and moon, the latter influence is toward causing the inclination to become less, in other words, to pull the equator down closer to the direction of their pull. The earth, however, is revolving rapidly, like a top. And like a top that leans from a vertical position and yet spins without falling, the earth resists this pull at the equator, and remains spinning and leaning at about the same inclination. But, as the peg of a leaning top slowly moves about in a circle, causing its equator to gyrate, so the pole of the earth and its projection in the sky move in a circle about the pole of the ecliptic. This does not cause a change of inclination in the axis of the earth, but causes the axis to gyrate, and this causes the equator of the earth and its projection in the sky to slowly move in relation to the ecliptic.

In determining this movement the vernal equinox, the point in the heavens where the sun crosses the celestial equator, is the station of importance. The constellations bear the same names as do the zodiacal signs. In fact, each evidently was traced among the stars pictorially to represent the influence of the sign bearing the same name. When the sun at the vernal equinox, the commencement of the zodiac, is found in the constellation Aries, the period is said to be in the Arian Age. When the sun at the vernal equinox is found to be in the constellation Pisces, it is said to be the Piscean Age. When the sun at the vernal equinox is found in the constellation Aquarius, it is said to be the Aquarian Age. These ages, and their lesser subdivisions, are found to influence the world at large. They denote that the sun and earth are in such relations to the stars, among which our whole solar system is rushing, that they transmit vibrations from this wider region, cut definite fields of energy, that influence the whole of humanity, giving direction to its evolution.

Having stated that each sign of the zodiac differs from the others in vibratory quality, it is next in order to discuss in what way this difference expresses itself. It manifests chiefly, but not exclusively, by modifying the tone quality of any planet located in the signs. In effect, the signs of the zodiac act as so many sounding boards from which the planetary vibrations are transmitted to us. Each planet has its own particular tone, which it always retains. From a musical standpoint, however, the tone C, or the tone G, or any tone within the octave, may be sounded on a wide variety of instruments. The chief vibratory rate will remain the same, but the tone quality will greatly vary. The same tone sounded on a violin has an entirely different effect upon the hearer than if sounded upon a bugle. The difference in the influence of the same planet when in one sign and when in another sign may be quite as great. The difference in such a musical tone, and the difference in the vibratory quality of such a planet, is due not to any change in the essential vibratory rate, but to the difference in the sounding boards from which they are sent forth. The zodiacal signs are the sounding boards that determine the precise resonance and quality of the planetary vibrations.

The signs, because they are keyed to particular vibratory rates, each transmit certain tones much more readily than other tones. They are thus each so sensitive to the vibratory rates of certain planets that they send forth a responsive tone even when the planet is not in the sign. This seems to be on the same principle that made it possible for Caruso to shatter a wine glass across the room by first finding the tone to which it was keyed and then singing this tone. Although the great singer was not touching the glass he caused it to respond with its own key, and finally caused this tone response to become so violent as to break the glass. Though acting as a sounding board, or medium of expression for the planet, each sign has its own key.

Likewise everything on earth has a key to which it vibrates. When it is discovered that some particular thing on earth, in the astral realm, or elsewhere, vibrates to the same key as that to which a zodiacal sign vibrates, the thing is said to be ruled by that zodiacal sign. In other words, when discussing occult subjects, if we are told that a certain thought, a certain color, a certain planet, a certain insect, or what not, is ruled by a given zodiacal sign, we are thereby apprised of the inner vibratory quality, or key, of the thing considered.

Such knowledge is of paramount importance to the occultist. Let us, therefore, without further delay, take up the study of the qualities that a vast amount of careful observation has shown to reside in each sign.

The first step in this direction should be to learn the names of the twelve signs, their correct order of sequence, and the particular section of the heavens occupied by each when the vernal equinox is on the eastern horizon. Also, as the signs are designated by symbols in astronomical and astrological tables and literature, such as almanacs and ephemerides, the symbol commonly used to denote each sign should be learned. This information may all be obtained from an inspection of the diagram on page 18 where each sign is associated with its symbol, and the correct sequence is denoted by numerals.

Now, although such a method of approach is not absolutely essential, for the sake of systematizing our knowledge of the signs, I find it convenient to have recourse to the magical quaternary rendered in the Bible of Jehovah, but known to initiates as Jod-He-

Vau-He. This is a formula that is found to be as valuable in the solution of occult problems as any formula of algebra is valuable in the solution of engineering problems. It is the formula, stated in terms of universal principles, that all life, action, and progress are the result of two interacting forces. The first term of the formula is a positive force. The second term is a negative, or reactionary force. The third term of the formula is the point of union where the two meet. The fourth term is the result of that meeting.

This formula, Jod-He-Vau-He, is universally applicable. Thus if we desire to apply it to economics, the radical political element of society becomes the Jod, or impelling force. The conservative, or reactionary, political element becomes the first He. The point of union, or Vau, is the political convention or ballot box. The final He, the product of the struggle, is the form of government resulting.

Now, by applying this ancient formula to the zodiacal signs, we find that they separate into four equal groups bearing just such relations to each other as the terms Jod-He-Vau-He suggest. As there are twelve signs in the zodiac, of course each of the four equal groups must contain three signs. And to designate that there are three signs in each group, the groups are called a Triplicity. There are, therefore, four zodiacal triplicities.

Each triplicity is named after one of the four ancient elements to which it corresponds. These were not considered elements in the sense that chemistry considers sulphur, mercury, carbon, and radium, elements. After all, in the true sense of the word, these latter are no more elements than the ancient fire, water, earth, and air; for all are composed of electrons and protons. Fire, to the ancients, was an abstraction by which the qualities of energy, zeal, and enthusiasm, whether expressed in a mineral such as sulphur, or in a vegetable such as mustard, or in a beast, such as a wildcat, might be designated. Water was used to express fluidity, receptivity, and germination. Earth was used to express coldness, concreteness, and solidity. Air was used to express vacillation, intangibleness, alertness, and fleetness. The terms, fiery, watery, earthy, and airy, were applied alike to objects, persons, and zodiacal signs.

Applying our magical formula, the fiery triplicity represents the positive, masculine Jod, even as the heat rays of the sun fall upon the world. The watery triplicity is the negative, feminine first He, such as the moisture that quenches the thirst of the parched desert. The earthy triplicity is the point of union of masculine and feminine forces, the Vau, as water and heat meet in the earth to germinate whatever seeds lie in the ground. The airy triplicity is the product springing from the union, the final He, the harvest brought forth in due season. As applied to man we may say that the union of enthusiasm and affection gestates as effort which results in intelligence. Or, stating it in terms of the four-fold sphinx, we may say that the energy of the Lion expresses through the sex of the Eagle, bringing about material incarnation and the plodding toil of the Bull, to the end of evolving the immortal Man.

In our study of the triplicities, and in our study of the signs as separate influences, we shall find it convenient to designate their relation to human types and human life. Not that their influence is confined to humanity, but because we are familiar with human qualities. When we learn their correspondences in terms of human character, it will then be no difficult task to determine their correspondences in other departments of nature. In considering the quality of a sign or group of signs as expressing through humanity I shall have special reference to people who have the Sun in their birth charts in these signs. The sign the Sun is in indicates in large measure the quality of the Individuality. However, the sign the Moon is in at birth largely determines the quality of the mentality, and the sign on the Ascendant determines largely the quality of the Personality. Furthermore, it should be understood that the sign the sun is in at birth is only one of many factors of the birth chart, all of which must be taken into consideration, and which may greatly modify the characteristics of the sign. Only certain deep-seated motives and impulses that underlie the character can be determined with certainty from the sun sign alone.

As there are different classifications of the zodiacal signs, so there are also different methods of classifying people. One of the oldest methods, and one that has distinct advantages as viewing them in relation to the zodiacal triplicities, is to divide them into four general groups. These groups have to do with the predominant temperament, classified as sanguine, lymphatic, bilious, and nervous.

The Fiery Triplicity embraces the signs, Aries, Leo, and Sagittarius. People born under this triplicity—meaning primarily the Sun being in this triplicity, as explained in Chapter 2, Course 10-1, *Delineating the Horoscope*—tend to the sanguine temperament. They possess self-reliance, enthusiasm, zeal, courage, daring, the ability to command others, and a love of activity. In the sense of being able to arouse in themselves and communicate to others initiative and enthusiasm, their characteristic quality is INSPIRATION.

The Watery Triplicity embraces the signs Cancer, Scorpio, and Pisces. People born under this triplicity tend to the lymphatic temperament. Their lives are largely centered in the home and affections. They are sympathetic, timid, dreamy, submissive, given to domestic life, receptive, yielding, mediumistic, and greatly influenced by their surroundings. In the sense that they are chiefly actuated by their feelings, rather than by carefully reasoned lines of conduct, their characteristic quality is EMOTION.

The Earthy Triplicity embraces the signs Taurus, Virgo, and Capricorn. People born under this triplicity tend to the bilious temperament. They are not given to bursts of enthusiasm, but express their ideas concretely, having the ability to apply themselves patiently to the affairs of this life and to turn all they contact to some material use. On the farm, associated with some industry, or managing some great corporation, they are toilers. In the sense of relying upon reason and the reports of the senses, and in interesting themselves in the affairs of earth that have value here and now, their characteristic quality is PRACTICALITY.

The Airy Triplicity embraces the signs Gemini, Libra, and Aquarius. People born under this triplicity tend to the nervous temperament. They are mentally alert, volatile, changeable, and socially inclined, desiring to live largely upon the mental plane. They are interested in education, literature, and art, are fond of conversation, and find pleasure in the exchange of ideas. In the sense of desiring refinement and intellectual culture, their characteristic quality is ASPIRATION.

We have now applied our magical quaternary formula in its broadest sense. Under this formula things are not only perceived to express our broad qualities, but viewed from a different perspective are seen to be a trinity. Then, turning them to be viewed still closer we perceive them also to be a duality; and finally, from another point of inspection, to be a unity. It will readily be seen, however, that these views offer no contradiction to the magical quaternary, for we perceive the three to be already contained in the four. The duad likewise appears in the quaternary. It is the principle of polarity. And, of course, unity expresses in the various separate parts of the four. Altogether, then, this magical formula, when its different perspectives are added together, completes the cycle and starts another; for 4-3-2-1 added together are 10.

As I illustrated briefly the application of the four factors of the magical formula I should not, I think, omit a brief illustration of the trinity. It is everywhere manifest, but that now most immediate to my consciousness is the sense of sight. How do we distinguish the objects we see? By a trinity. Straight lines are positive. Curved lines are negative. These are two factors. The third is their point of union, the combination of straight and curved lines. As you look at this page its meaning is conveyed to you by a trinity, straight lines, curved lines, and their mutual relation to each other. The lines themselves, as well as every object and every picture, is conveyed to the consciousness by still another trinity. There are light spaces and there are shadows, or colored spaces. Neither alone has significance. It is only when dark spaces and light spaces have the third element, the point of union, that form is perceived.

Now it is true that in considering a trinity it may be turned so as to be viewed as a quaternary or as a duality or as made up of unities. As a quaternary we might say that the fourth factor in the above illustration is the printed word or the form as perceived, just as we could properly consider straight lines and curved lines as the duality, and each as a unity. But this is changing the perspective, and in no way vitiates the usefulness of the trinity. Matter, for instance, exists in three states; gaseous, liquid, and solid. Likewise the zodiacal signs fall into three groups; the movable signs, the mutable signs, and the fixed signs.

We have already seen that there are four triplicities. Each triplicity contains three signs, and each of these signs expresses the element to which the triplicity corresponds in a different state of activity. This different state of activity is called the Quality of the sign. Triplicity and Quality must not be confused. There are four triplicities—fire, water, earth, and air—but there are only three Qualities—Movable, Mutable, and Fixed.

The signs of the Movable Quality are Aries, Cancer, Libra, and Capricorn. They express the nature of each of the four elements in the highest state of activity. Matter in the gaseous state, though chemically the same, is far more active and possesses different qualities than when in the liquid or solid state. People, also, born under the movable signs, are active, energetic, and given to change; even as gas generates power and finds it easy to move in various directions little hindered by gravitation. They break the trails that others follow, and start the enterprises that others finish. The natives of Aries pioneer in daring enterprises and adventure. Cancer people pioneer in home building and in foods. Those born under Libra pioneer in literature, art, and social affairs; while those belonging to the sign Capricorn are pioneers in business and industry. The signs of the movable quality produce people who are PIONEERS.

The signs of the Mutable Quality are Gemini, Virgo, Sagittarius, and Pisces. They express the nature of each of the four elements in a medium state of activity. Matter in the liquid state, though possessing the same chemical elements as when gaseous or solid, is more subject to gravitation and less aggressive in its chemical action than when gaseous; but more active and yielding, and less given to permanence than when in the solid state. The mutable signs are a happy medium between the excessive activity of the movable signs and the stubborn resistance of the fixed signs. Liquid cannot force its way through an aperture as easily as can gas, but once a channel has been established it quickly follows the line of least resistance. People born under the mutable signs seldom break trails, but follow on the heels of the pioneers. As liquid conforms to the object with which it is in contact, so mutable people are the most adaptable of all. The signs of the mutable quality produce people who seldom originate an enterprise. They are the DEVELOPERS.

The signs of the Fixed Quality are Taurus, Leo, Scorpio, and Aquarius. They express the nature of each of the four elements in the lowest state of activity. Matter in the solid state is rigid, durable, and unyielding. People born under the fixed signs are quite as unbending, firm, and resistant. Solids find difficulty in altering their form and location; and people belonging to the fixed signs are strongly attached to their customary environment, their customary manner of doing things, and their customary methods of thought. They have great resistance to pressure of all kinds, strong endurance, plodding perseverance and the ability to give close attention to detail. They are not originators, and not enthusiastic developers; but when development has reached a high degree, they work out details that constitute improvements. The signs of the fixed quality produce people who are PERFECTERS.

Now we found when considering sight, that it could be viewed as a trinity from two different perspectives. We also find that the signs of the zodiac may be viewed as a trinity in two different ways.

In addition to the Quality, which, as we have seen, relates to the state of activity of the signs belonging to each of the four elements, there is also the matter of precedence in the zodiac of the signs belonging to each of the four elements. Thus of the fiery signs, one of them occurs first in the zodiac, another second, and another third, in the order of their succession, commencing with the vernal equinox. It is found that this matter of precedence in the zodiac has much to do with the etherealization of the spiritual and mental forces as expressed through the signs. This manifests itself in human life chiefly in regard to whether the motive for action is largely internal or largely external.

Reverting to our comparison of the radiations from the planets to definite musical tones, and of the signs to sounding boards from which these tones are reverberated; we might class the fiery signs as stringed instruments, the watery signs as the liquid chimes, the earthy signs as the booming drums, and the airy signs as the wind instruments. We might even go further, and class the movable signs as those instruments that take the celestial treble, the mutable signs as those that take the ripe tenor, and the fixed signs as those that sound the rolling bass. Yet, even with such a classification, there would still remain to be considered the particular tone quality of each instrument, by which it could be discerned from other instruments, even from those playing the same tones and employing a similar method, as the tone of a guitar may be distinguished from the same tone on a violin.

This tone quality is thus still further elaborated by considering the sign's precedence in the zodiac, compared to other signs of the same triplicity. This designation is called its Degree of Emanation. The first sign of a triplicity in the zodiac belongs to the first degree of emanation, the second sign to the second degree of emanation, and the third sign to the third degree of emanation.

The signs of the First Degree of Emanation are Aries, Taurus, Gemini, and Cancer. People born under these signs act from motives that chiefly spring from their own feelings, ideas, and inward yearnings. When expressing themselves they tend to externalize their own inner nature with LIBERTY.

The signs of the second Degree of Emanation are Leo, Virgo, Libra, and Scorpio. People born under these signs act from their own feelings, ideas, and inward yearnings, tempered by a full consideration of what other people feel, think, and advise. When expressing themselves they tend to externalize their own inner nature with MODIFICATION.

The signs of the Third Degree of Emanation are Sagittarius, Capricorn, Aquarius, and Pisces. People born under these signs act less from their own feelings, ideas, and inward yearnings, than from ideas and attitudes that have reached them from without. When expressing themselves they tend to externalize their own inner nature with RESERVE.

We are now ready to consider the zodiacal signs as a duality. Commencing with Aries as the first positive and masculine sign, every alternate sign is negative and female. The positive, masculine, electrical signs are: Aries, Gemini, Leo, Libra, Sagittarius, and Aquarius. The negative, feminine, magnetic signs are: Taurus, Cancer, Virgo, Scorpio, Capricorn, and Pisces.

To complete our view of the zodiacal signs we have yet to discuss them as a unity. We have considered them as a quaternary, as a trinity, as a duality; and now we must consider them as a unity, each sign as a sounding board of specific tone quality for celestial vibrations.

Aries

Pictured among the constellations by the Ram, is the first sign of the zodiac. It belongs to the element fire; hence we expect it to be energetic, courageous, and daring. It is a movable sign, comparable to burning gas, therefore not to be confined, or dictated to by another. Belonging to the first degree of emanation, it is little influenced by precedent or environment. It is a masculine sign, and assertive. In human anatomy it rules the head. As the first sign of the zodiac it represents birth, as ruling the brain it signifies perception. Aries people express a fiery will, a militant power, executive ability, imperious leadership, and the dauntless pioneer spirit. They are ambitious, enterprising, forceful, combative, self-willed, keen, independent, active, and desirous of being in command. Impulsive and fiery, yet even in apparent rashness they are guided by intellect. All the world seems new to Aries people. Their dominant idea is I AM.

Taurus

Traced among the stars as the Bull, is the second sign of the zodiac. It belongs to the element earth; hence we expect it to be industrious, patient, and practical. It is a fixed sign, comparable to frozen earth, therefore, stubborn, immovable, and conservative. Belonging to the first degree of emanation it bows little to the opinions of others, and usually has a tendency to become interested in psychic phenomena. It is a feminine sign, reserved and not intruding. In human anatomy it rules the ears, the base of the brain, the neck, and the throat. Commands are received through the ears, and Taurus people are obedient servants, careful, plodding, and self-reliant. The motor nerves spring from the region ruled by Taurus, hence we find them persistent and untiring workers. They have pronounced powers of discrimination, will wait a long time for plans to mature, are secretive, and possess enormous reserve energy. They are strongly attracted to money, and express themselves by its use. Capricorn is the organizer of industry, Virgo the engineer, and Taurus the perfector of its details and the custodian of its wealth. The dominant idea is I HAVE.

Gemini
Pictured in the sky by the Twins, is the third sign of the zodiac. It belongs to the element air, consequently is volatile, intellectual, and changeable. It is a mutable sign, comparable to liquid air, therefore possessing wonderful powers of mental expansion and a constant flow of ideas expressed through conversation or writing. Belonging to the first degree of emanation, it is not bound so much by material motives as actuated by the desire for mental expression. It is a masculine sign, able to exert considerable initiative. In human anatomy it rules the hands, arms, and upper respiratory system. The hands, as organs of execution, are dual, and Gemini people are remarkable for both executive ability and versatility. They usually are interested in several things at once, and change their occupation often. They have a fondness for learning, are restless, dexterous, sensitive, skillful, and intuitive; and ever on the alert to learn the "Why" of things. Their dominant idea is I THINK.

Cancer
Represented in the heavens as a Crab, is the fourth sign of the zodiac. It belongs to the element water, therefore is sensitive, receptive, and timid. It is a movable sign, comparable to fog, subject to whims, moods, and varying changes, not to be confined in a single environment, but possessing unusual freedom to alter its own position. Belonging to the first degree of emanation, its moods and yearnings are expressed pronouncedly. It is a feminine sign, but makes up with tenacity its lack of aggressiveness. In human anatomy it rules the seat of nourishment, the breasts, bosom, lower lungs, and stomach. Cancer people absorb ideas and conditions and after digesting them are capable of diverting them to their own use. They are not active physically, but are intensely active assimilating and redistributing sense impressions. Mediumistic, reflective, dreamy, mild of temper, emotional, very domestic, they respond to kindness, sympathy, and approbation, are fond of publicity, and are influenced by their sur-

roundings. The dominant idea is I FEEL.

Leo
Designated in the firmament by a Lion, is the fifth sign of the zodiac. It belongs to the element fire, therefore is impulsive, passionate, and daring. It is a fixed sign, comparable to hot metal, dominating, ambitious, and resolute. Belonging to the second degree of emanation, its actions spring from the emotions rather than from the intellect. It is a masculine sign, possessed of unbending dignity. In human anatomy it rules the heart and back. Leo people are sympathetic, warm-hearted, candid, forceful, and fond of honors and high office. They are not so active as Aries people, but possess great determination to rise, and strive to rule through strength and stability rather than through alertness and activity. Their ideas are large and majestic, despising petty effort, and in striving to reach higher states often overreaching. Unlike Aries people, when aroused emotionally they do not count the cost. The dominant idea is I WILL.

Virgo
Emblazoned above as the celestial Virgin, is the sixth sign of the zodiac. It belongs to the element earth, therefore is practical, industrious, and worldly. It is a mutable sign, comparable to liquid earth, such as mortar, binding together what others quarry, selecting materials furnished by other people and placing them in their proper order. Belonging to the second degree of emanation, it is neither so independent of environmental influences as Taurus, nor so dependent upon them in regard to its completeness of expression as Capricorn. It is a feminine sign, preferring arbitration to combat. In human anatomy it rules the navel and bowels. Virgo people are intensely discriminative, even as the function of the intestines is to assimilate the food required by the body. The constant process of analysis for the purpose of discrimination inclines them to be critical. Intensely active mentally, they have a faculty for acquiring knowledge, being studious, scientific, mentally alert, ingenious, witty, fluent, discerning, and ever seeking "How" desired results may be accomplished. The dominant idea is I ANALYZE.

Libra
Pictured along the pathway of the sun as the Scales, is the seventh sign of the zodiac. It belongs to the element air, therefore is changeable, bright, and socially inclined. It is a movable sign, comparable

to the gusts of wind on an April day, pioneering in the arts and in social affairs. Belonging to the second degree of emanation, it combines idealism with worldly motives. It is a masculine sign, adaptable, but not submissive. Libra people are easily influenced by others, but quickly regain their equilibrium. They are sensitive, refined, sympathetic, artistic, neat, particular, dislike unclean work, and are inordinately fond of approbation. Lovers of justice, peace, and harmony, they are kind, generous, and affectionate, finding social relations extremely important, and a partner often essential to their happiness. They are fond of music and entertainment, are courteous, and desire to make many friends, yet in their affections are somewhat changeable. The dominant idea is I BALANCE.

Scorpio

Pictured among the constellations by a scorpion, is the eighth sign of the zodiac. It belongs to the element water, hence has strong emotions and is domestically inclined. It is a fixed sign, comparable to water crystallized through great pressure rather than through lowered temperature, and therefore capable of exerting tremendous force, boiling the moment it finds an avenue of escape. At once unyielding, yet it is capable of exerting immense pressure upon its environment. Belonging to the second degree of emanation, it moves more with the world's mental current than athwart its flow. It is a feminine sign, very receptive and meditative. In human anatomy it rules the generative organs and procreative attributes. Scorpio people have a never failing fund of ideas and resources, and an abundant life giving magnetism. They are proud, secretive, reserved, jealous, energetic, ingenious, strong willed, determined, enterprising, and skillful, making good surgeons, doctors, chemists, scientists, and mechanics. Their dominant idea is I DESIRE.

Sagittarius

Represented among the stars as a Centaur, is the ninth sign of the zodiac. It belongs to the element fire, hence is energetic, hasty, and enthusiastic. It is a mutable sign, comparable to molten metal, aggressive and impulsive, but not dominating. Belonging to the third degree of emanation, its actions are largely shaped by what other people think proper and in good taste. It is a masculine sign, positive and forceful. In human anatomy it rules the hips and thighs, which are the foundation of volition and locomotion. Sagittarius people are a happy medium between Aries people, who are ruled by their heads, and Leo people, who are ruled by their hearts. They love outdoor sports, are loyal, patriotic, generous, free, ambitious, charitable, and jovial. Frank, outspoken, self-reliant, they are great travelers, are very conservative, have prompt decision, and the ability to command others. The dominant idea is I SEE.

Capricorn

Traced in the constellations as the Goat, is the tenth sign of the zodiac. It belongs to the element earth, hence is practical, industrious, and acquisitive. It is a movable sign, comparable to dust, adapting itself to every requirement to gain its ends; persistent, subtle, and ambitious. Belonging to the third degree of emanation, it acts largely from external motives. It is a feminine sign, gaining its point by cunning rather than by force. In human anatomy it rules the knees. Capricorn people are humbly submissive to those in power, and unceasing in their efforts to gain power that others may bend the knee to them. They are diplomatic, good organizers, ever alert to take advantage of circumstances or the weakness of the other people, are careful, cautious, frugal, and insistent, with thoughtful, serious, reflective minds. Their dominant idea is I USE.

Aquarius

Shown in the vault of heaven as the Man, is the eleventh sign of the zodiac. It belongs to the element air, hence loves the society of others and the interchange of ideas. It is a fixed sign, comparable to crystallized air, is the most practical of all the airy signs, and the one possessing the most continuity. Belonging to the third degree of emanation, its actions are greatly influenced by its external environment. It is a masculine sign, extremely assertive. In human anatomy it rules the ankles, the active power of locomotion. Aquarius people are very progressive, usually possessing ideas more advanced than their companions. They are inventive and scientific, pleasant, friendly, quiet, patient, determined, faithful, cheerful, sincere, easily influenced by kindness; artistic, refined, have strong likes and dislikes, are greatly interested in education and new discoveries, and like nothing better than an argument. The dominant idea is I KNOW.

Pisces

Represented among the constellations as the Fishes, is the twelfth sign of the zodiac. It belongs to the element water, hence is dreamy, mystical, and romantic. It is a mutable sign, comparable to water, mirroring like a lake its environment, moved by every motion near it. Belonging to the third degree of emanation, it tends to become all things to all people. It is a feminine sign, listless and negative. In human anatomy it rules the feet, the foundation of the human temple. Pisces people, though imaginative and dreamy, have the ability to flow into such grooves of the world's affairs that they usually acquire the material things necessary for comfort. They are idealistic, sensitive, mediumistic, prone to worry, peaceable, sympathetic, prudent, modest and often lack self-confidence. No other sign has such extremes of temperament and ability; for Pisces people will be found both on the height and in the depth, and some of them are successful in almost every line of human endeavor. The dominant idea is I BELIEVE.

EXPRESSION OF PLANETS THROUGH THE HOUSES

A planet in a house, or ruling it, influences the events of the department of life mapped by that house in the following manner:

Sun, expresses through VIGOR.

Moon, expresses through FLUCTUATION.

Mercury, expresses through THOUGHT.

Venus, expresses through GRATUITIES.

Mars, expresses through STRIFE.

Jupiter, expresses through ABUNDANCE.

Saturn, expresses through POVERTY.

Uranus, expresses through ECCENTRICITY.

Neptune, expresses through ILLUSION.

Pluto, expresses through COERCION.

DEPARTMENTS OF LIFE RULED BY THE HOUSES

Each Mundane House maps the particular section of man's astral body, or the particular section of the world's astral form, the inner-plane activities of which determine what happens in one department of life. The departments of life thus mapped are as follows:

First House: personality, health, the body.

Second House: money, personal property.

Third House: thoughts, studies, short journeys, relatives.

Fourth House: father, real estate, home, end of things.

Fifth House: speculation, children, love affairs, entertainment.

Sixth House: work, illness, food, employees.

Seventh House: marriage, partnership, public, open enemies.

Eighth House: death, inheritance, taxes, money of others.

Ninth House: publicly expressed opinions, books, religion, long journeys.

Tenth House: the job, business, honor, reputation.

Eleventh House: hopes, friends, acquaintances.

Twelfth House: secret enemies, disappointments, astral entities.

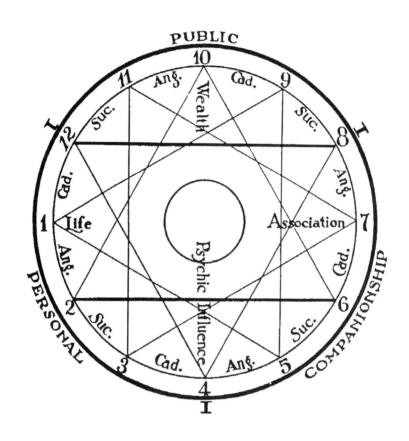

SYMBOLS

☽ Moon

☿ Mercury ☉ Sun ♃ Jupiter

♀ Venus ♄ Saturn

♂ Mars ♇ Pluto ♅ Uranus

♆ Neptune

Chapter 3 _____

Mundane Houses

_____

P LANETARY vibrations not only must have a point of departure, but also, if they are effective, must have a place of reception. A tone reverberating from the sounding board of one of the zodiacal signs must reach the earth in order to affect the destiny of the inhabitants of the earth. To do this it must penetrate the astral field associated with the earth. The direction from which such a planetary vibration reaches a given spot on the earth determines the relative direction of movement of the astral field penetrated, and also the amount of astral field through which it must pass. These two factors, it has been ascertained by observation, determine the department of life which the vibrations will influence. To ascertain the volume of planetary vibrations reaching the earth from given directions, and the departments of life they influence, is our object in the study of Mundane Houses.

In preceding lessons I have compared the planetary vibrations to musical tones. In fact, I know of no better designation for them than planetary tones. Each planet sounds its own tone. The zodiacal signs I have compared to sounding boards from which these tones resound. The tone is modified, not in its essential vibratory rate, but in tone quality, by the sounding board, or zodiacal sign, from which it reverberates. Furthermore, musical tones and planetary tones have both a point of departure and a place of reception; and the place of reception of planetary tones, so far as we are concerned, is the earth, acting as a grand auditorium.

In most auditoriums, due to distances from the instruments, to obstructions that may intervene, and to other acoustic factors, tones are not heard in the same volume and with the same precision throughout all its sections. The earth as an auditorium is unique; for the various musical instruments, the zodiacal signs, are ranged completely around the outside of it. Nevertheless, as in most auditoriums, the relation of a particular point in it to the positions where tones are being sounded, modifies the tones at the place of reception. That is, tones coming from one direction are stronger and clearer than tones coming from another direction, because they have less of the astral field of the earth to penetrate, and are less interfered with by its rotation due to the turning of the earth on its axis.

It will thus be seen that persons occupying different portions of the terrestrial auditorium-situated at different stations on the face of the earth-will not hear the tones from the celestial instruments with the same clarity. At any given time some may be more favorably located than others for the reception of certain tones.

Because in the case of the earthly auditorium it seems to be the thickness or thinness of the astral field of the earth at a given point, together with its movement, that determines the ease with which planetary tones reach a given point, we may compare the terrestrial auditorium to a building the walls of which are of varying thickness. At certain intervals there are doors, and at other intervals there are windows. Thus the musical instruments ranged around the outside easily find access for their tones through the wide-open doors; find access with less ease through the windows; and reach the interior only with great difficulty through the denser portions of the walls. It is to map these sections of varying resistance that we have recourse to a diagram of the Mundane Houses.

Thus to map the amount of wall thickness, and the tone modifications due to earth rotation, at any given spot on the surface of the earth; that spot is taken as the center, about which, from west to east, is circumscribed a circle. This circle, commencing at the eastern horizon, is then divided into twelve equal segments. Mundane means pertaining to the earth. A house is a dwelling place. A Mundane House, then, is the dwelling place of a celestial influence at any moment of time, considered solely from the point on the earth where the influence is received. Each of the twelve equal segments of the circle about the earth from west to east is a Mundane House.

A clearer conception of the Mundane Houses may be had by facing the south and imagining one's self the hub of a great wheel, the circumference of which passes directly from the horizon in the east, on the left, under one's feet around to the horizon in the west, on the right, from thence directly overhead, and back to the eastern horizon again. Let one then imagine this great wheel to possess twelve spokes radiating into the sky from the point where one stands as a center, these spokes equally spaced about the wheel. Such a wheel accurately pictures the twelve houses of a horoscope, the dividing line between two houses, called a House Cusp, being represented by each spoke.

The first spoke in this great wheel is occupied by the horizon directly to the east of where one stands. The eastern horizon, then, is the cusp of the First House. This is a very important point in a horoscope, and because it is at this place that the planets rise from below the horizon into view it is called the Ascendant.

The opposite horizon, directly to the west of the observer, representing the seventh spoke of the great wheel, is the cusp of the Seventh House. Because it is the point where the planets sink from view below the western horizon it is called the Descendant.

The point directly beneath one's feet, representing the fourth spoke of the great wheel, is the cusp of the Fourth House. Because it is the lowest point it is called the Nadir.

The point directly overhead, the zenith, representing the tenth spoke of the great wheel, is the cusp of the Tenth House. This is also a very important point in a horoscope, for it is here that a planet reaches its greatest elevation. It is called the Mid-Heaven, or more often abbreviated from its Latin equivalent, Medium Coeli, and merely termed the M. C.

These four spokes divide the earthly auditorium into four quadrants. At sunrise the sun is exactly on the cusp of the Ascendant. At midnight the sun is exactly on the cusp of the Nadir. At sunset the sun is exactly on the cusp of the Descendant. At noon the sun is exactly on the cusp of the M. C. (See diagram, page 18).

Because we of northern latitudes must look south to view the sun or a planet when it is on the M. C., the cusp of the Tenth House is also called the South Point. And because the Nadir, abbreviated from the Latin Imum Coeli as I. C., is opposite the South Point, it is sometimes called the North Point. The four points, Asc., M. C., Desc., and Nadir, are the strongest points in a horoscope in the sense that a greater volume of energy reaches the earth from a planet when it is located near one of these points than when it is located in any other section of the heavens. This is not difficult to demonstrate experimentally. It is as if at other stations there were walls of varying thickness, but at these points the doors were wide open so that the planetary tones may enter the auditorium without interference.

Now as the zodiacal signs are each thirty degrees in extent, and the houses of the horoscope are also of thirty degrees expanse, at first thought it might be assumed that the equivalent of one sign, or thirty degrees of the zodiac, always occupies exactly one Mundane House. This certainly would be the case if the circle of Mundane Houses coincided with the zodiac. However, it does not coincide with the zodiac. Except at the equator the Mundane Houses are to the north or to the south of the mean position of the zodiac. The effect of thus being to the north or to the south of the equator in its extreme influence is familiar to us in the accounts of arctic explorers who witness a midnight sun.

In such a case the degree of the zodiac occupied by the sun does not, during the twenty-four hours, pass into any of the six houses below the horizon. This midnight sun, as well as the phenomenon of six months daylight followed by six months darkness near the poles, is the result not merely of the observer occupying a high latitude, but also to the incident that the zodiac is inclined at an angle of over 23 degrees to the equator. That is, even at the equator, the zodiacal signs rise diagonally. The further to the north or to the south of the equator the observer moves the more diagonally do the signs rise. Thus in north temperate latitudes in summer, the sun appears on the horizon, when it rises, well north of east of the observer, and as it moves toward noon it swings up and to the south. The farther north the observer goes, the farther to the north the sun appears to rise in summer, until finally, in extreme north latitudes, it fails to set, merely circling around the north horizon from the west to the east at night without disappearing.

Now if you draw two parallel lines an inch apart, and then measure the distance between them diagonally instead of straight across, you will find that the diagonal line is much more than an inch. In fact, the more the diagonal inclines to the parallel lines the longer it must be. Without entering into a technical explanation of the matter, it will be seen that if the zodiac rises diagonally, as it were, that it is necessary for some of the Mundane Houses of thirty degrees extent to contain more than thirty degrees of the zodiac. Furthermore, being true circles, if the zodiac is diagonal to the Mundane Houses at some points, relative to the zodiac the Mundane Houses are diagonal to it at other points. To state it more precisely, as there are 360 degrees in the zodiac and 360 degrees in the Mundane Houses, if more than thirty degrees of one section of the zodiac occupies one house, less than thirty degrees of some other section of the zodiac must occupy some other house.

A technical explanation of the reason why, in making a chart of the heavens, more often than not some Mundane Houses will hold more than thirty degrees of the zodiac and others less than thirty degrees of the zodiac, would be out of place here. I trust, however, these remarks will give a general idea why it is that more than one zodiacal sign may, and often does, occupy one house of the horoscope. As the basis on which the Tables of Houses commonly employed are constructed is that each shall contain precisely thirty degrees, I trust also that it will be clear that so long as we employ such tables, each Mundane House must be exactly thirty degrees in extent, irrespective of the number of degrees of the zodiac it holds.

To make a map of the Twelve Mundane Houses the student should draw a circle and bisect it with a heavy horizontal line from left to right. This horizontal line represents the horizon, and the half of the circle above this line represents the visible portion of the heavens-all that is above the horizon. The half of the circle below this line represents the portion of the heavens that is invisible due to being below the horizon.

Next the circle should be bisected by a vertical line. All to the left of this line is eastward, and all to the right of this line is westward, from the observer. As to see the planets and the zodiac we face the south, the top of the map is south; just the reverse of a geographical map. The four quadrants now mapped by the two intersecting lines should each be divided by two radii from the center of the map, thus dividing each into three equal sections. This gives a circle divided into twelve equal segments (See diagram, page 18), which should be numbered, commencing with the segment just below the eastern horizon as the First House, the next segment below it as the Second House, etc.

That energies of tremendous power, hitherto quite unrecognized, are pelting the earth day and night from the regions of space, has been demonstrated by the discovery in 1925 of the Cosmic Ray. That such a force-so powerful that were its volume to increase it is believed it would constitute a serious menace to life upon the earth-should remain undiscovered so long, leads to the inevitable conclusion that there may be numerous other energies reaching and influencing the earth as yet to be brought within the ken of material science. And one willing to investigate will find that a planet sending its rays to the earth through a certain one of the Mundane Houses has an effect upon a different department of life than if its rays were received through any of the other houses.

Consider for a moment that most of us feel differently than at other times when the sun is in the Third House-from midnight to about 2 a.m. Physical vitality is low at this period, and more people die-so medical statistics state-during this interval than during any other. While the sun is in the Second House-from about 2 a.m. to near dawn-not merely the physical forces are sluggish; but the courage is low and the mind depressed. It is the zero hour. Yet with the coming of dawn, and from then to sunrise-while the sun is in the First House-there is a general awakening of life energies the world over. Immediately after sunrise there is a temporary lull, and yet a very different influence again in the period just preceding noon.

I am here merely calling attention to conditions that are familiar to all who observe closely. The rotation of the earth causes rays from the planets to meet with different densities of astral field, or with the astral field moving differently, as they reach the earth through the various Mundane Houses. In some manner this resistance offered by the earth's astral field-under the particular motion that obtains in each respective house-causes whatever planetary energies that pass through the house to have a specific affinity with the section of a person's astral body where are stored the thought-cells relating to some special department of life. All the mechanical steps by which vibrations coming through one house influence chiefly one special department of life may not be theoretically clear. But for that matter neither is it mechanically clear why the roots of a plant grow away from the sunlight and the stalk of the plant toward it. Yet we can prove they do so; and it is not a more difficult task to prove-using the birth chart of the first person at hand-that planetary energies reaching the earth through a certain Mundane House have an affinity for a certain department of life. The consideration of this relation between the Mundane Houses and the department of human life affected through each, is the next matter to engage our attention.

As we found the magical formula, Jod-He-Vau-He, of great assistance in studying the zodiacal signs, we shall also find it advantageous to apply it in a similar manner to the Mundane Houses. Even as the signs were found to separate into four equal groups of three signs each, so likewise the Mundane Houses separate into four trinities.

The Trinity of Life embraces the First, Fifth and Ninth Houses. The first house influences the constitution and vitality. The fifth house influences the life of the offspring. The ninth house influences the life in relation to religion and philosophy. This trinity corresponds to the fiery signs of the zodiac.

The Trinity of Psychism embraces the Fourth, Eighth, and Twelfth Houses. The fourth house influences the home and the end of life. The eighth house influences death and inheritance. The twelfth house influences sorrows and imprisonment. This trinity corresponds to the watery signs of the zodiac.

The Trinity of Wealth embraces the Second, Sixth, and Tenth Houses. The second house influences personal property. The sixth house influences labor and servants. The tenth house influences business and honor. This trinity corresponds to the earthy signs of the zodiac.

The Trinity of Association embraces the Third, Seventh and Eleventh Houses. The third house influences the thoughts and the brethren. The seventh house influences partnership and marriage. The eleventh house influences hopes and friends. This trinity corresponds to the airy signs of the zodiac.

Next we must consider the houses as of three different Volumes; each volume embracing four houses.

The Angular Houses are the First, Fourth, Seventh, and Tenth. These are of the strongest volume. It is as if there were wide open doors about the earthly auditorium at these stations, through which the full volume of planetary influence may enter unimpeded. They are called angular because their cusps, being directly upon the eastern and western horizons and upon the zenith and nadir, are the lines dividing the heavens into quadrants.

The Succedent Houses are the Second, Fifth, Eighth, and Eleventh. They are of moderate volume, as if there were but small windows in the earthly auditorium at these stations, through which celestial tones may enter only in reduced amounts. They are called succedent because they succeed, or follow, the angular houses.

The Cadent Houses are the Third, Sixth, Ninth, and Twelfth. These are of the least volume, as if at these stations about the earthly auditorium there were thick walls through which the heavenly tones penetrate only as muffled sounds. They are called cadent—meaning to "fall away"—because they fall away from the other houses both in volume of influence and in position.

Now we found that the zodiacal signs were divisible not only into Three Qualities, but also into Three Degrees of Emanation. Likewise, we find that the Mundane Houses are divisible into Three Volumes; also into Three Societies.

The Personal Houses embrace the Twelfth, First, Second, and Third. They influence personal sorrows, the personal body, the personal property, the brethren and personal thoughts. These houses have to do with the private life.

The Companionship Houses embrace the Fourth, Fifth, Sixth, and Seventh. They influence the companionship in the home and at the end of life, the companionship in pleasure and with children, the companionship in work and with servants, and the companionship in partnership, in marriage, and in meeting the public. These houses have to do with closely contacting people.

The Public Houses embrace the Eighth, Ninth, Tenth, and Eleventh. They influence the public life through deaths and legacies, through advertising and public utterances, through reputation and credit and through friends. These houses have to do with matters that become widely known.

As a Duality, the Mundane Houses may also be viewed in two different ways. They may be considered in relation to the facility with which their influence gains recognition. And they may be considered in relation to the waxing or the waning of their power. The Six Houses above the Horizon-Seventh, Eighth, Ninth, Tenth, Eleventh, and Twelfth-are positive and tend to the ready expression of any influence found in them in such a way that it gains recognition. The Six Houses below the Horizon-First, Second, Third, Fourth, Fifth, and Sixth-are negative and tend to the development of whatever influence is found in them in secrecy. The Six Houses on the East side of the chart-Tenth, Eleventh, Twelfth, First, Second, and Third-tend toward increase, and whatever influence is found in them inclines to further development. The Six Houses on the West Side of the chart-Fourth, Fifth, Sixth, Seventh, Eighth, and Ninth-tend toward decrease, and whatever influence is found in them inclines to dissolution.

Having now discussed the Mundane Houses as a quaternary, a trinity, and as a duality, to complete our magical formula, 1-2-3-4 equals 10, we have yet to consider them as a unity.

The First House belongs to the trinity of life. It is an angular house; consequently transmits energy of the strongest volume. It is a personal house, related to the private life. Being below the horizon its influences tend to develop in secret; but as it is on the east side of the chart they develop persistently. It influences the health, the personal appearance, the temperament, such matters as cause changes in the form or location of the person; and in general the personality through which the character must express.

The Second House belongs to the trinity of wealth. It is a succedent house; consequently transmits energy only in moderate volume. It is a personal house, related to the private possessions. Being below the horizon these possessions are not open to public inspection; yet any influence expressing through this house tends to development. The tenth house represents the business, and the sixth house the labor involved; but the second house represents the fruits of these in terms of cash and other personal property.

The Third House belongs to the trinity of association. It is a cadent house; consequently transmits energy very weakly. It is a personal house, related to the private thoughts. Being below the horizon these thoughts may never be expressed to others; but any influence in this house tends toward development. It influences the thoughts, which are the mental associates; the brethren, neighbors, writing, short journeys, correspondence, and education.

The Fourth House belongs to the trinity of Psychism. It is an angular house; consequently transmits energy of the strongest volume. It is a companionship house, relating to those in the home. Being below the horizon its influences tend to be kept from the public, and as it is on the west side of the chart they have little power of growth. This house influences the parentage, the father in particular, the home and general domestic environment, inherited tendencies, real estate, hidden things, and the condition at the close of life. These things, as exerting a powerful influence on the unconscious life, are of psychic import.

The Fifth House belongs to the trinity of life. It is a succedent house; consequently transmits energy only in moderate volume. It is a companionship house, relating to the companionship of children and the companionship in pleasure. Being below the horizon its influence is not heralded to the public, nor do we expect any influence here to undergo great development. It rules broadly the life of the affections, of the children, and of the pleasures; governing speculation, amusements, offspring, and love affairs.

The Sixth House belongs to the trinity of wealth. It is a cadent house; consequently transmits energy very weakly. It is a companionship house, relating to servants and to those with whom one works. Being below the horizon any influence here tends to be kept secret, and as it is on the west side of the chart there is little opportunity for growth. It influences broadly those things that assist or hinder the acquisition of wealth, such as assimilation, illness, labor, inferiors, and servants.

The Seventh House belongs to the trinity of association. It is an angular house, consequently transmits energy of the strongest volume. It is a companionship house, relating to partnerships and marriage. Being above the horizon its influences tend to gain wide recognition; although there is little growth from them. It governs the relations with the public, partnerships, open enemies, lawsuits, and marriage.

The Eighth House belongs to the trinity of psychism. It is a succedent house; consequently transmits energy only in moderate volume. It is a public house, and the things it influences are kept secret with great difficulty. They do not, however, tend toward any great development. It influences the relations to the public's money, and to the money of the partner: also the relations to the dead, both their psychic influence and the inheritance from them. In addition to such legacies it also influences the conditions surrounding the person's death.

The Ninth House belongs to the trinity of life. It is a cadent house; consequently transmits energy very weakly. It is a public house, having to do with the public expression of opinions. Being above the horizon the things it influences tend to gain wide recognition. They do not, however, tend to continued development. This is the house ruling advertising, publishing, dreams, long journeys, philosophy, religion, and the public expression of ideas.

The Tenth House belongs to the trinity of wealth. It is an angular house, consequently transmits energy of the strongest volume. It is a public house, relating to the credit and honor. Being above the horizon there is public recognition of the things it influences. These things are subject to much development. It influences the mother, the trade or profession, the business qualifications, superiors, credit, reputation, and the esteem in general with which one is held by others. It thus greatly influences material success.

The Eleventh House belongs to the trinity of association. It is a succedent house; consequently transmits energy only in moderate volume. It is a public house, and the things it influences are widely known. Being above the horizon there is full recognition of all its affairs, and they are subject to persistent development. Its associations are occasional rather than constant. It governs acquaintances, friends, hopes, and wishes. In particular it influences the attitude toward, and the benefit that may be derived from, acquaintances.

The Twelfth House belongs to the trinity of psychism. It is a cadent house; consequently transmits energy very weakly. It is a personal house, and its affairs are kept as secret as possible, although being above the horizon the things it influences nevertheless gain some recognition. They also tend to persistent development. It influences secret enemies, sorrows, disappointments, restrictions, limitations, imprisonment, unseen forces, and the relation to astral entities.

Now let us apply the magical quaternary, Jod-He-Vau-He, to the planets. They are naturally divisible into such a quaternary because their energies affect four different phases of human life. Thus there are Vital Planets, Intellectual Planets, Social Planets, and Business Planets. The vital planets are the Sun and the Moon. The intellectual planets are Mercury and Uranus. The social planets are Venus, Mars, Neptune, and Pluto. The business planets are Saturn and Jupiter.

The trinity into which the planets are divisible is based upon whether their usual effect upon human life is Harmonious, Discordant, or Convertible. The harmonious planets are Jupiter and Venus. The discordant planets are Saturn and Mars. The convertible planets are Sun, Moon, Mercury, Uranus, Neptune, and Pluto. These convertible planets are not essentially harmonious or discordant, but may become either through the aspects received from other planets.

As a duality the planets are divisible into those that are electric and positive, and those that are magnetic and negative. The electric and positive planets are Sun, Mars, and Jupiter. The magnetic and negative planets are Moon, Venus, Saturn, Neptune and Pluto. Uranus is neutral and electromagnetic. Mercury is either positive or negative according to its association with other planets, being but the mediumistic transmitter of the positiveness or the negativeness of the other planets.

We have now discussed the planets as a quaternary, a trinity, and a duality, and to complete our 1-2-3-4, it remains to treat them as a unity.

1. The Sun is a vital planet, and a convertible planet, exerting either a harmonious or a discordant influence according to the aspects received from the other planets. He is electric, masculine, and positive, hence in his influence he is majestic and commanding. In human anatomy he rules the heart, the vital center of life. This gives us an insight into his character; for as the heart is the dominant physical organ, its pulsations being the source of circulation which makes life possible, so he rules the electrical energies on which the vitality depends. In his influence over the mind he rules the group of mental factors designated as the Power Urges, embracing pride, firmness, approbativeness, conscientiousness, and self-esteem. His influence is greater than that of any other planet, being proud, grand, firm, unbending, kindly, gracious, paternal, considerate, moderately liberal, and controlling. His nature is best expressed in one word as VITALITY.

2. The Moon is a vital planet, and a convertible planet, exerting either a harmonious or a discordant influence according to the aspects received from the other planets. She is magnetic, feminine, and negative, hence her influence is plastic and mediumistic. In human anatomy she rules the fluidic system of the body, the foundation of the health and general constitution.

This gives us an insight into her character; for as the fluidic system digests, assimilates, and distributes nutriment, so the Moon rules the assimilation of mental food by the astral brain, or unconscious mind. Her influence is cool, yielding, and formative, ruling the constitutional magnetism which markedly influences the health. In her influence over the mind she governs that group of mental factors designated as the Domestic Urges, embracing time, tune, sublimity, and philoprogenitiveness. Her influence over the strength of the constitution and the general state of the health is marked. She is changeable, negative, dreamy, inoffensive, and lacking in force. Her nature is best expressed in one word as IMPRESSIONABLE.

3. Mercury is an intellectual planet, and a convertible planet, exerting either a harmonious or a discordant influence according to the aspects received from the other planets. He is electric and positive when associated with electric planets, and magnetic and negative when associated with magnetic planets. In human anatomy he rules the tongue, brain, and nervous system. This gives us an insight into his character; for as the nervous system carries messages to and from the brain to all parts of the body, so Mercury acts as the messenger for the influence of other planets. As the tongue is the most used

organ in the expression of thought, Mercury rules writing, talking, traveling, and the manner in which the mental ability is expressed. Thus while the Moon governs the Mentality, Mercury indicates the Ability, and the channels used, in giving the mind outward expression. And as there are afferent, or ingoing nerves, and efferent, or outgoing nerves; so Mercury influences both perception and expression. He has dominion over the perceptive and comparative group of mental factors designated as the Intellectual Urges, embracing eventuality, language, calculation, and the recognition of size, weight, form, and color. He is witty, quick, ingenious, intelligent, scientific, volatile, voluble, bright, enterprising, changeable, and persuasive. His nature is best expressed in one word as PERCEPTION.

4. Venus is a social planet, and a harmonious planet. She is magnetic, feminine, and negative, hence yielding and submissive. In human anatomy she rules the skin, venous system, and internal generative functions. This gives us an insight into her character; for as the skin is the organ through which feeling is experienced, so Venus is coy, shy, and sensitive. The venous system gently yields to the arterial pressure and carries the blood back to the heart, and Venus seeks the line of least resistance. The internal generative functions carry out the work of reproduction, and Venus, the planet of love, reproduces through the various arts the mental creations. In social life she inclines to affection and attraction. In her influence over the mind she rules that group of mental factors designated as the Social Urges, embracing, affection, friendship, mirthfulness, conjugality, and inhabitiveness. She is cool, moist, pliable, amiable, receptive, clinging, convivial, harmonious, and artistic. Her nature is best expressed in one word as MILDNESS.

5. Mars is a social planet, and a discordant planet. He is electric, masculine, and positive, hence aggressive and penetrating. In human anatomy he rules the external sexual organs, the muscles, and the sinews. This gives us an insight into his character; for as the muscles and sinews are the organs of physical activity, so does Mars ever tend to rapid expansion and active effort. As the sexual organism is the seat of strongest desire, so does Mars have dominion over the animal appetites and passions. In social life he inclines to desire and strife. In his influence over the mind he rules that group of mental factors designated as the Aggressive Urges, embracing amativeness, destructiveness, combativeness, and alimentiveness. He is the exact antithesis of Saturn, being diffuse, hot, impulsive,

rash, headstrong, and assertive. He is devoid of fear and timidity, is sharp, energetic, thoughtless, free, fierce, intrepid, and unrelenting. His nature is best expressed in one word as ENERGY.

6. Jupiter is a business planet, and a harmonious planet. He is electric, masculine, and positive, hence dignified and bold. In human anatomy he rules the liver and the arterial system of the body. This gives us an insight into his character; for as the arterial blood distributes warmth and nourishment to the whole body, so Jupiter ever tends to generosity, warmth, and gentle expansion. He is neither the rigid ice of Saturn, nor the fierce fire of Mars, but a genial radiant warmth, imparting happiness to all. In his influence over the mind he rules that group of mental factors designated as the Religious Urges, embracing benevolence, good cheer, veneration, hope, reverence, and spirituality. Whatever good Jupiter brings seems to come freely as the result of good will and good luck. Saturn gains in business through careful systematic effort, while Jupiter gains through patronage and favor. He is cheerful, generous, benevolent, magnanimous, just, charitable, honest, and discriminative. His nature is best expressed in one word as JOVIALITY.

7. Saturn is a business planet, and a discordant planet. He is magnetic, masculine, and negative, hence timid and retiring. In human anatomy he rules the bones, cartilage, and spleen. This gives us an insight into his character; for as the bones are the most solid portions of the body so does Saturn tend to the practical and concrete. As the spleen is a reservoir of electrical energy, so does Saturn try to collect and hoard the treasures of the earth and the treasures of the mind. In his influence over the mind he rules that group of mental factors designated as the Safety Urges, embracing secrecy, acquisitiveness, covetousness, causality, and comparison. He collects the various perceptions that are ruled by Mercury and synthesizes them into conceptions. He thus has rule over the reflective powers and the selfish sentiments. Whatever good comes from his influence is the result of carefully laid plans, plodding effort, subtlety, craft, and cunning. He dislikes to take the initiative, preferring to remain in the dark and accomplish through deception rather than through force. He is solitary, cold, reserved, melancholy, repentant, and fearful. His nature is best expressed in one word as CRYSTAL-LIZATION.

8. Uranus, the higher octave of Mercury, is an intellectual planet, and a convertible planet, exerting either a harmonious or a discordant influence according to the aspects received from the other

planets. He has no sex, and is electromagnetic, alternately attracting and repelling, hence particularly unreliable where the affections are concerned. In human anatomy he rules the electromagnetic body. This gives us insight into his character; for as the electromagnetic body is ordinarily imperceptible to the physical senses, yet is the dynamic energy of the body and the source of personal magnetism, so does Uranus direct and control the electrical energies and confer the ability to understand and utilize the occult forces of nature. In his influence over the mind he rules that group of mental factors designated as the Individualistic Urges, embracing independence, originality, inventiveness, and unconventionality. The moons of Uranus travel in a reverse direction to those of the other planets, except Neptune, hence he influences to take the reverse view of life from that commonly accepted, and is thus a radical; and he also inclines to look away from the physical to the things of the astral plane, having a strong influence over clairvoyance and intuition. He is thus the Inspirational ESP planet. He is abrupt, erratic, independent, sudden, penetrative, original, occult, scientific, unconventional, and progressive. His nature is best expressed in one word as DISRUPTIVE.

9. Neptune, the higher octave of Venus, is a social planet, and a convertible planet, exerting a harmonious or a discordant influence according to the aspects received from other planets. He is magnetic and negative in nature. In human anatomy he rules the astral body. This gives us an insight into his character; for as the astral body is molded by every desire, so does Neptune feel every mental current and psychic influence. As the astral body has the power of leaving the physical body, so does Neptune often depart from the practical and give its attention to unrealizable ideals. His dreamy and mediumistic qualities may lead to fantasy and the belief in grand hopes that are never realized. His moons, like those of Uranus, revolve about him in the reverse direction of those of the other planets. And his influence is to direct the mind from the sordid and the material to lofty spiritual ideals which when received in suitable soil tend to the development of the conditions and qualities that prove of greatest possible value to the human race. In social life he brings romantic attachments and platonic friendships. In his influence over the mind he rules that group of mental factors designated as the Utopian Urges, embracing certain high phases of majestic and utopian ideals, and the ability to bring into the realm of objective consciousness what has been seen, felt, heard, and other-

wise experienced in the astral world. Neptune is the Feeling ESP planet. He is the promoter of worldly schemes to gain wealth without work. He is subtle, impressionable, psychic, emotional, mild, pleasant, theoretical, and fanciful. His nature is best expressed in one word as VISIONARY.

10. Pluto, the higher octave of the Moon, is a social planet, and a convertible planet, expressing either a harmonious or a discordant influence according to the aspects received from other planets. Like the number 10, which starts a new numerical cycle, Pluto is a transitional influence, and more than any other planet may express in either of two diametrically opposite qualities. He may express positively and electrically, but his more common influence is negative and magnetic. In human anatomy he rules the spiritual body. In his influence over the human mind he rules that group of mental factors designated as the Universal Welfare Urges. They relate to groups, cooperation, the inner-plane, hidden forces, inversion, the inside of things, mass production, and to aggressive spiritual activity. The Lower-Pluto forces are drastically insidious and destructive, the Upper-Pluto forces are the finest and most spiritual of all. Not the individual who instigates the action, but the victim of coercion, has this planet prominent. To such events as he attracts, or to which he contributes, he adds a drastic quality. Pluto is the inner-plane planet and the planet of Transition ESP. His nature is best expressed in one word as COOPERATION.

I have now discussed in some detail Mundane Houses and Planets, and in chapter 2 the zodiacal signs were considered. To complete our magical formula, Jod-He-Vau-He, the fourth factor, that of aspects, must also be considered. But as these aspects are explained in Chapter 3 of Course 1, *Laws of Occultism,* and are fully considered in Chapter 2 of Course 8, *Horary Astrology,* I shall here merely enumerate them.

1. The Conjunction aspect is formed when two planets occupy the same zodiacal degree. It has an influence comparable to the Sun, being very powerful, convertible in nature, and either harmonious or discordant according to the planets making it. It is the aspect of PROMINENCE.

2. The Semi-Sextile aspect is formed when two planets are 30 degrees apart in the zodiac. It has an influence comparable to the Moon, being mildly harmonious. It is the aspect of GROWTH.

3. The Sextile aspect is formed when two planets are 60 degrees apart in the zodiac. It has an influence comparable to Venus, being cheerful, bright and strongly harmonious. It is the aspect of OPPORTUNITY.

4. The Square aspect is formed when two planets are 90 degrees apart in the zodiac. It has an influence comparable to Mars, being energetic, forceful, violent, destructive, and strongly discordant. It is the aspect of OBSTACLE.

5. The Trine aspect is formed when two planets are 120 degrees apart in the zodiac. It has an influence comparable to Jupiter, being jovial, fortunate, constructive, and harmonious in the highest degree. It is the aspect of LUCK.

6. The Inconjunct aspect is formed when two planets are 150 degrees apart in the zodiac. It has an influence comparable to Neptune, being slightly separative in action, slightly harmonious between harmonious planets, and slightly inharmonious between discordant planets. It is the aspect of EXPANSION.

7. The Semi-Square aspect is formed when two planets are 45 degrees apart in the zodiac. It has an influence comparable to Mercury, being vacillating and somewhat inharmonious. It is the aspect of FRICTION.

8. The Opposition aspect is formed when two planets are 180 degrees apart in the zodiac. It has an influence comparable to Saturn, being slowly separative, coldly disintegrative, and discordant in the highest degree. It is the aspect of SEPARA-TION.

9. The Sesqui-Square aspect is formed when two planets are 135 degrees apart in the zodiac. It has an influence comparable to Uranus, being sharply disruptive, sudden, and somewhat discordant. It is the aspect of AGITATION.

10. The Parallel aspect is formed when two planets occupy the same degree of Declination, which, like the number 10, is a different plane of influence. It has an influence comparable to Pluto, adding a drastic quality to the effect of other aspects. It is also similar to the conjunction, though more persistent and less precise in action. It is the aspect of INTENSITY.

Chapter 4 _____

Mission of the Soul

_____

THE PURPOSE of this lesson is to give information about the human soul such as will serve as a working basis for those who are struggling to attain Self-Conscious Immortality. To begin with we must know just what the soul is, and what it is not. Then it will be advantageous to know just how it was formed, and how it continues to grow. And finally, as the end which is of paramount value to each individual, the method will be outlined by which Self-Conscious Immortality can be won.

The reflective mind will hardly deny that self-culture is an object of highest import to man. Externals are of value only when there is an inner capacity to appreciate them. Of what value, for instance, is anything to that which has no consciousness? The struggle of life in all its forms seems to be but the effort to acquire, retain, and express, consciousness. Lower creatures cling to life, and the hope of immortality dwells within each human breast. It is the climax and crowning glory of evolution, the longed-for goal of every aspiring heart.

Such being the case, we are warranted in studying thoroughly how this desired end may be reached. And we can do no better in this at the start than to consider the principles underlying other great attainments. Take, for example, the stupendous achievements of the present age along industrial lines. These are without exception, founded upon man's increased ability for exhaustive detailed research, together with his ability to combine the innumerable factors revealed by such research into an efficient plan of action. Whether he be a builder of warships, skyscrapers, power plants, or railroads, his success depends primarily upon his grasp of all the factors and principles involved, and upon his ability to combine them in such a way as to give a true picture of the means to be used to attain striven-for results.

The Formula of Success

The primary requisite for success in any enterprise, then, is adequate knowledge. That success may actually be attained, adequate knowledge must be followed by adequate action based upon this knowledge. If we were to require a formula for success in any effort we might state it thus: The best and most certain results in any line of endeavor can be attained only by one clearly comprehending all the various factors and principles involved who, after becoming familiar with methods, and having decided upon some definite aim, carefully plans a course of action and persistently adheres to it in the face of all obstacles, making adaptations only to meet changing environment, or as the dictates of matured experience demands.

If the human heart craves immortality, as it universally does, this is an end to be attained. As such it is subject to the formula just stated. That is, it can be attained more surely if its various factors are clearly comprehended and serve as a basis for persistent endeavor.

What is it, then, that may be immortal? The soul. But what is the soul? This we must ascertain. Suppose we begin the explanation by saying that thought implies a thinker. If anything is known, there must be a knower. The individual who thinks and feels logically concludes he has an existence. Furthermore, in some manner, he feels sure of the identity of the "I" of yesterday with the "I" of today. There is something about the "I" of today which is the same as, and something which is different from, the "I" of yesterday. What it is that is the same, and what it is that is different, only analysis will reveal.

Now back of consciousness resides the energy that expresses consciousness. Back of life in manifestation is the energy that expresses life. Back of all expressions of that which ultimately becomes the mind of man is energy. We are unable to think of the universe as nonexistent. Its energies must have been present in some state throughout the entirety of the past. In other words, the universe is manifesting today a potentiality that has always been present; for energy is not derived from nothingness.

Likewise, back of all expressions of individual consciousness and form there is a potentiality. This potentiality, this energy that expresses itself through consciousness and form, finally expressing through the human form as the mind of man, was not derived from nothing. It is a potentiality as eternal as the potentiality behind the universe; for while energies express in different forms, one of the most stable natural laws is that of conservation of energy, the law that there is no more and no less energy in the universe today than there was in the infinitely distant past, or than there will be in the infinitely distant future. The "I", therefore, that does not change, the "I" that we feel existed farther back than we can remember, and that we can hardly imagine as not existing in the future, is the potentiality which activates our existence. It is usually referred to as the ego.

As to our consciousness, it cannot be said to be changeless. On the contrary it continually changes. I do not mean merely that the objective consciousness is aware of different things at different times, but that because new experiences are each day and each hour added to the total of our consciousness, that consciousness, in its entirety, is in a state of flux. Yet we identify ourselves with our states of consciousness. Insofar as we do this the "I" of today is different from the "I" of yesterday. The totality of these states of consciousness is the soul.

We have no experience of energy not associated with substance, and no experience of consciousness not associated with substance. Nor are we justified in assuming that energy and consciousness are possible apart from some kind of substance. In fact, the human mind is incapable of thinking of a condition in which substance is absent. Of course, there are substances much finer than matter; but for energy to express, or for consciousness to be present, each must be associated with substance. When energy expresses as consciousness in association with substance, the substance is spoken of as the form, or body.

The Sole Attribute of the Ego Is Potentiality

From the fact that we now exist, no new energy ever being created, it is logical to assume that we each have at least potentially always existed. That is, the potentiality which we call the ego never had a beginning and never can have an end. But states of consciousness are more than potentialities, they are the result of specific activities. Until the ego inaugurated these specific activities there was no consciousness, consequently no soul. The ego must always have existed, but the soul only came into existence as the result of definite activities of the ego. The soul, therefore, probably has not always existed.

When that potentiality which we now call the ego inaugurated the specific activities that resulted in the first gleam of consciousness, the activity was a movement of substance, and the consciousness itself was a special kind of motion in substance. Thus, the moment there was consciousness there was also a form. Consciousness, in fact, must be nothing, or it must be a movement in some kind of substance. Logically it cannot be nothing. And as movement in substance has form, and the soul embraces states of consciousness, the soul is ever associated with a form. Consequently, as soon as the ego has the first rudiments of a soul it also has at least the rudiments of some kind of a body.

Before it had a soul, the ego existed as a potentiality, as an eternal spark of the infinite; co-eternal with Deity. But there came a time when it initiated specific activities. Hermetic tradition holds that this was due to the love vibrations of angelic parents occupying a plane interior to the spiritual. That is, the undifferentiated potential spark of Deity was drawn to the celestial realm and there given birth by beings occupying that realm. At least it is certain that its potentialities were given a definite trend, otherwise there would have been no soul.

As soon as specific activities commenced, there also developed an awareness of these activities. The ego came in contact with its environment, which was that of the celestial realm, and began to have states of consciousness as the result of its experiences. These states of consciousness of the celestial realm developed a soul sphere, a sphere of consciousness organized in celestial substance, about the ego. But the trend of activity given the ego by its divine progenitors was of immensely greater scope than could find expression in the infinitely tenuous realms of celestial life. Its potentialities were directed to penetrating and conquering, that it might develop deific attributes, the lower realms of existence known as the spiritual plane, the astral plane, and the material plane.

Hermetic tradition holds that due to laws governing such processes, the celestial soul sphere—the organizations of consciousness in celestial substance surrounding the ego—is unable to communicate energy to, or receive energy from, substances grosser than that of the highest spiritual realm. Because celestial substance is so much finer than the others, there are insufficient points of contact to transmit motion. A familiar illustration of this principle is the transmission of energy by radio. This energy has not sufficient points of contact with most physical objects to affect them. To cause motion in physical substance requires special conditions. And the ego, so Hermetic tradition holds, is able to impart its energies and directing power to substance coarser than the finest spiritual substance, only under conditions of a certain kind.

These conditions, under which the ego, operating from the seventh state of the spiritual world, is able to contact lower spiritual substance and thus transmit energy to still coarser astral substance and physical substance, are believed to be the polarization of its energies into two separate channels of flow; related to each other as positive and negative, masculine and feminine. The states of consciousness evolved by the ego, then, in the spiritual world, the astral world, and the physical world, represent two separate organizations. Each of these organizations of consciousness is a soul.

We are familiar with somewhat similar organizations in the study of the structure of the atom. Each atom of matter, according to the chemistry of today, is a positive nucleus of energy about which revolves one or more negative charges of energy, or electrons. Each different element has a definite number of electrons revolving around the positive nucleus. In the case of man, according to the Hermetic conception, the constant factors are a single ego, about which revolve two human souls.

The potentialities of the ego, therefore, are directed, due to the trend given it by its angelic parents, to developing these two, male and female, souls.

This development is accomplished through experience. In fact, the only possible way of developing consciousness is through experience. All knowledge, as was illustrated in detail in Chapter 1, Course 1, *Laws of Occultism*, necessarily rests upon experience. This will the more readily be understood when it is realized that consciousness is a perception of relations, and that apart from an awareness of relations there can be no consciousness. But in order for there to be such awareness, relative conditions must be contacted. These conditions are present only in association with substances. That is, it is possible to evolve consciousness only through contact with substances that in some manner display differences; for only through the awareness which perceives likeness and unlikeness is there consciousness.

To Become Conscious the Ego
Must Contact Relative Existence

It will now be perceived that if the ego is to emerge from its state of unconsciousness, in which it has neither wisdom nor feeling, its sole attribute being potentiality, it must contact the plane of relative existence; it must contact the region of substances; it must contact conditions that provide it a basis for comparison. Let us get this clear: Either the ego remains in a state of absolute ignorance and absolute insensibility—a state that is better than complete annihilation only because it contains the potentiality of becoming the other alternative—or it must gain experience through contact with relative conditions. If the ego is to possess the qualities that make for an existence that can be considered worth while, it must have experience with various grades, or conditions, of substances.

What, then, is necessary to contact substance, and what is necessary to utilize the perceptions gained by such contact? To contact substance, there must be an attractive power. To utilize impressions gained from substance there must be developed a mechanism of consciousness. The soul, then, develops a dual function: It acquires the power to attract substance, and it evolves the quality of retaining, in specially organized substances, the consciousness of its experiences with other substances.

In order that these experiences should be varied enough to constitute worth-while knowledge, to constitute a consciousness of some scope, it is obligatory that the ego, through the soul, should contact numerous conditions and states of substance. These are to be found in form. Thus it is that the various forms of life with which we are familiar are all being used as vehicles, by which souls gain experience and so widen their knowledge.

The scope of experience that may be had in association with any single form is limited. Therefore, the soul developed the power of attracting one form and using it as a vehicle of experience for a time, and then attracting another form. Yet before the second form can be utilized as a vehicle, the first form must be left, or repelled. But the universe is not filled with ready-made forms. Consequently, in order that it may have just the form to meet its temporary requirements, the soul developed the power to mold forms.

To state this conception in a somewhat more concrete way, let us think of the ego as the source of energy. The ego has no wisdom, no consciousness, until it has experience; for consciousness is the result of experience. When it does commence to have experiences, these experiences are recorded as states of consciousness; and the sum total of all these states of consciousness comprise the two souls of one ego. That is, according to the Hermetic tradition, each ego, in so far as substance coarser than the finest spiritual substance is concerned, has two different organizations of consciousness, two souls.

But the function of a soul is not merely to record states of consciousness. A state of consciousness is not nothingness, therefore, it must be something. And it can only be an organization of energy in some kind of substance. It may be an organization of energy in astral substance, or if fine enough, in spiritual substance, or if of still greater sublimation, even in substance interior to the spiritual. But it is always an organization of energy, and as such has the power to perform work. That is a function of all energy; to perform work. And the energy of consciousness has the power to attract substance and mold itself a form, or body, that corresponds to that consciousness.

It uses this form to gain still further experiences, and these experiences are recorded and become a portion of the soul. Because it now has a more complex organization than before, it is able, after repelling a form, to attract another that is of greater complexity. Experiences in successive forms enlarging its states of consciousness, which are additional organizations of energy, enable it later to attract a body of still higher organization.

The Soul Has a Dual Function

Thus it is that the soul has a dual function: that of attracting, molding, and repelling the various forms that give it experience; and that of recording these experiences. Consciousness, which records these experiences, implies an adjustment of internal relations to external relations, and this process of continuous adjustment we call conscious life.

But even as there can be no consciousness, knowledge, or wisdom, except that based upon experience with forms; so there can be no love, no attraction, other than through association with form. The former are perceptions of relations; but these relations which are perceived are simply the feelings of various degrees of attraction and repulsion. Without the perception of relations there are no attractions and repulsions. Yet these, when they become sufficiently complex, we term love. As love is dependent upon perceptions of relations, and these are dependent upon experience, it will be seen that apart from experience with relative conditions there can be no love, and no knowledge of love.

There can be no consciousness of attraction, no love, except that developed through experience with forms that have various qualities. Not only then, does the soul exercise the power of attracting and repelling forms, but its ability to attract and repel forms depends upon its experiences in so doing; for each experience adds to the consciousness. It should be plain, therefore, that without the experiences of external life, without the experience of functioning through various forms in some sort of substance, there would be no soul, and there could be neither feeling nor knowledge, neither Love nor Wisdom.

Life, likewise, implies change. We cannot think of life apart from alterations of the internal structure. Yet movement is impossible apart from substance. Consequently, the ego could have no life, other than being merely a potentiality, except through association with form. Without the experience of functioning through various forms in some sort of substance there could be no love, no wisdom, and no Life.

Why We Are Here

To the question so often asked as to why we are here, why man must pass through experiences, some of which seem heart-rending, the answer is plain: Without some such experience there could be no Life, there could be no Love, and there could be no Wisdom.

We cannot perceive the light, except we have had experience with varying degrees of its intensity; and if we have had some experience with darkness, we the more readily appreciate the light. We can have no knowledge of the good, unless we have had some experience with that which is less good; and if we have had some experience with that which we call evil, the good is the more appreciated. Sweetness, to the sense of taste, is only perceived by comparison with things less sweet. It takes the sour, such as lemon, to bring out in proper contrast the sweetness of honey. In fact, the wider the range of experience the clearer the perception of qualities and values. Without some such experiences with form as we are familiar with there would be no life, no consciousness, no knowledge, no love. It is impossible to imagine how life, wisdom, and love could be developed, or could exist, without some such chain of experiences as those with which we are familiar.

As to the why of existence itself, that is, the why of the potentiality manifesting through the universe of form, we are not called upon to explain it. We cannot conceive of a condition in which existence is lacking, nor have we had any experience that suggests such a condition ever was possible. It is quite enough, then, for the human mind to attempt to explain how existence acts and is conditioned, without attempting to commence from nothingness, which is logically impossible, and show how all that exists was derived from this unthinkable, impossible, abstraction. But if we commence with a potentiality, such as the ego undoubtedly is, it is not difficult to trace the steps by which the soul must have gradually developed until it finally functions through the body of man.

As I have already shown in some detail, the attractive power that for convenience I call Love and the consciousness that for convenience I call Wisdom, are developed only through experience with form. I mean here that all activity and life are due to the principle of attraction which to generalize I refer to as Love, and that consciousness results from the activities so engendered. Such consciousness, in all its forms, I generalize under the term Wisdom. Furthermore, the feeling of attraction and the consciousness are intensified in proportion to the contrasts in experience. For instance, if we have just tasted something sweet, we are the more conscious of, and the more repelled by, the taste of something bitter. In fact, the wider the contrast is between experiences, the stronger they tend to impress themselves upon consciousness and the stronger they attract or repel. And the more varied the experience, the more shades of consciousness, the more discrimination possible; and the more shades of feeling, the wider the sensations and emotions.

Therefore, if the soul is to develop power; which depends upon its strength to attract and repel, upon Love; and if it is to develop knowledge, and not remain semi-conscious, it must have experiences of as wide contrast and of as great variety as possible. Contrast means strong impressions and strong desires. Variety means discrimination and fine shades of feeling. A creature without these is not alive in the full sense that man is alive.

The greatest contrast of which we know is that between spirit, or still finer substance, and matter. And the greatest variety of which we know is the countless forms on the physical, the astral, and the spiritual planes.

If, therefore, the soul is to develop its powers, there is no means that we can imagine which would be so effective as its association with the various forms of the physical, the astral, and the spiritual worlds; for these forms offer the widest possible contrast of which it is possible to conceive. They, therefore, offer the greatest opportunity to develop the attributes of attraction and repulsion; the greatest opportunity to develop feeling, to develop that which becomes Love.

And if the soul is to develop discrimination, there is no means that we can imagine which would be so effective as its association with the various forms of the physical, the astral, and the spiritual worlds; for these forms offer the widest possible variety of which it is possible to conceive. They, therefore, offer the greatest opportunity to develop the attributes of perception and comparison; the greatest opportunity to develop knowledge; to develop that which becomes Wisdom.

That the soul may acquire Self-Consciousness it must attain Wisdom. Life, however, depends also upon love; for love is the power that attracts and holds together whatever form the soul occupies. If the soul is to be immortal it must develop sufficient love, sufficient attractive power, to build such forms as are necessary for its imperishable existence. Love and Wisdom are the essential factors of Immortal Life.

Because there is no conceivable way by which the soul can acquire love and wisdom except through varied experiences in form, the cycle through which the soul passes, from spirit to matter and from matter back to spirit; living in countless forms in each of the three realms; is called by initiates, "The Cycle of Necessity." That is, this cycle of experiences in various forms is a necessity if the soul is to acquire the love and wisdom which alone make possible Self-Conscious Immortality. The mission of the soul, therefore, is to acquire Love and Wisdom to the end that Self-Conscious Immortality may be attained.

The Cycle of Necessity

Now let us trace the soul in its Cycle of Necessity. It is first differentiated in the highest state of the spiritual realm. It then possesses neither consciousness nor feeling; but is supplied by the ego with energy, and by the ego is given a specific trend. This specific trend is determined by the love vibrations of its angelic parents that brought about the ego's differentiation. That is, such ego with its two souls is a part of universal society, differing from all other egos. In universal society, as in all meritorious organizations, there is division of labor. Nature moves toward specialization, each specialized part performing a definite function. Therefore, the soul impelled on its cyclic journey is given that trend which offers it the opportunity to develop such attributes as it requires if it is ultimately to fill its proper sphere as a useful member in the cosmos.

It therefore attracts about itself, as the result of the energy supplied it by the ego, a form of spiritual substance of the highest state. Its experiences in this form give it some slight consciousness; being energy, when it repels the present form gives it additional power to attract another form of slightly greater complexity. Its experiences in the second form give it the consciousness, and the attractive ability, later to attract a third spiritual form of higher complexity still.

Its attractive power and its subjective consciousness increasing, it gradually gains the ability to attract forms of grosser spiritual substance; and after much experience living subjective lives in the lowest grade of spiritual substance, it finally gains the power to draw about itself an astral form. This process continues in the astral realm. These forms inhabited on the astral plane are termed elementals. As soon as the experiences in one astral form have been assimilated, this form is repelled and the organizations of energy thus gained enabled it to attract a still more complex, and a still more dense form, until finally a time is reached when the soul has enough energy, or love power at its command, as the result of its experiences in spiritual and astral forms, to enable it to attract about itself a physical form. This is the first objective experience; it becomes incarnated in a mineral.

The mineral form of life is the lowest rung on this Jacob's Ladder by which the soul descends from, and ascends to, heaven. Carried on the mineral life wave it enters the zone of the planet where its first expression of external life is to be experienced. By its power of love, which is the outcome of its experiences upon the descending arc of its cycle, it attracts to itself the attributes which constitute a crystal of matter. This initial crystal is the simplest form of mineral. The attributes expressed by it are due to the polarizing power of the soul.

After undergoing its cycle of life in the form of the lowest mineral, the soul begins to lose affinity with it, and finally, as the result of repulsion, passes into the astral realms. The mineral is dead. After a period of astral life, however, the soul, by the power of its accumulated love, attracts a new form and undergoes incarnation; this time in a mineral a step higher in the scale of evolution. Having reaped and recorded the experiences of one form, the soul is impelled, by the restless ego in search of wisdom, to exert its power to attract and mold a higher and more complex form. Thus it evolves, step by step, in its first evolutionary state, through the various kinds of mineral life.

From the highest mineral form, the monad is carried into the astral zones corresponding in astrological quality to the next planet of the septenary chain, there to undergo a period of subjective life. This is the second evolutionary state. Finally it is carried forward by the life wave and becomes incarnated, as its third evolutionary state corresponding to the next planet, in the vegetable kingdom. Here the action of love and wisdom evolves it still more rapidly by means of successive births and deaths. The lowly lichen forms but a step, and as it dies the soul, by its inherent power of love, attracts to itself a higher form of plant life, evolving rung upon rung on the ladder of evolution, ever attracting, evolving, and perfecting forms for more perfect and complex expression; and finally repelling them for those still higher in the gamut, until at last it blooms as the blushing rose.

From the highest type of plant life the evolutionary life wave of the solar system carries the impersonal monad to its fourth evolutionary state, astrologically corresponding to the next planet of the septenary, to undergo another cycle of assimilation in the astral spheres. Thence, after a period of subjective gestation, it passes to the fifth evolutionary state, corresponding astrologically to the next planet, to enter what has now become the animal life wave. Through attraction, or love, the soul becomes incarnated in the lowest form of animal life. Through love, which is the expression of accumulated wisdom, it molds the form it temporarily occupies. Then, after its cycle of experience in this form, the animal dies, and the soul, having more complex needs, or desires, attracts to itself a still more complex form, evolving, through the power of love, or desire, this form to meet as nearly as possible the requirements of its environment.

Having exhausted the realms of animal life, and ever impelled by the restless energy of its ego to seek new and more complex experiences, it passes from the region of its animal experiences to undergo another period of subjective assimilation in the astral spheres, the sixth evolutionary state, corresponding astrologically to the next planet in the septenary; thence onward to the seventh evolutionary state, in which it reaches the climax of incarnated perfection.

In the scheme of universal law the seventh state is always that of action and completion insofar as expression is concerned. The seventh condition is always a synthesis of the six preceding, and constitutes the point of transition to a new octave of existence. So, in the seventh evolutionary state from its commencement, the soul undergoing the Cycle of Necessity attains the estate of manhood, where it recapitulates in a single life all the various states through which it has passed, and attracts to itself the perfect form which has an exact correspondence to every plane, state, and center of life in the universe.

At this point in its journey, for the first time, and as the result of the accumulated impersonal wisdom gathered through the power of love, or attraction, it becomes self-conscious. It is no longer an impersonal being impelled forward by inner and to it unaccountable yearnings. It is now a self-conscious entity endowed with all the responsibility of a morally free agent; a responsibility varying in individual cases, being proportional to the ability and the opportunity.

The Structure of the Soul

At every step of the wearisome journey there has been the dual action of the soul. It has ever recorded for the ego the perceptions which constitute its store of wisdom, and these states of awareness for the sake of convenience we can classify as thoughts. Thus also all experiences which the soul has had may be classified according to the kind of thought-elements they contain. And even as the protoplasm of physical life exists as cells, so does the psychoplasm composed of thought-elements exist within the finer forms as thought-cells and thought structures they have built. And these exercise the power of love to attract, evolve, and finally to repulse forms.

The form which the soul occupies at any given moment of its journey is determined by the strength and direction of its love. The strength and direction of its love at any given time is dependent upon its accumulated experience, which I here term wisdom. Thus the soul has been gaining in both Love and Wisdom at every step of its cyclic journey, and these two are the Isis and Osiris of all life.

An acorn falls to the ground, germinates, and becomes the giant oak. No materialist can say, in spite of chromosomes and chromospheres, just what and where is the power that molds the oak into its unyielding form. Remove any single root or branch and the oak still lives. Cut it down in its prime and a new growth springs up. We cannot say the oak is another tree if it loses a branch, nor can we point out the exact locality in space where the real oak lives; yet we tacitly admit that there is a real oak that molds the physical to its present form and structure, a something that shapes it thus rather than to the form of a pine.

In time the tree dies, its physical form disintegrates, and the particles which have formed its body pass into other forms. What, think you, has become of the force that molded these particles to its specific structure? Do you think it is lost? No so! It has passed onward again to mold a form, this time a higher form that will meet its more advanced need of expression. It never again becomes the oak, for evolution is the law of objective existence. It is never, therefore, attracted to the same form, but always to one still more perfect, one more advanced, even though slightly, in the scale of being.

The scale of being is complete in the divine form of man. In man form reaches its highest state of perfection insofar as mundane life is concerned. The gamut of being embraced within the human form is a miniature representation of the entire universe. Reaching down from the realms of undifferentiated unconscious spirit to the dense mineral there is a perfect gradation of substance, and a perfect scale of life forms.

From mineral back to God extends Jacob's Cyclic Ladder, each rung upward a more perfect form, a more complex expression of Love and Wisdom. Each ascending step in this progressive movement is a more perfect form. Through form alone can the soul gather from the tree of the knowledge of good and evil, and only after partaking of this fruit, which embraces its experiences, is it also able to partake of the tree of life; of undying love. In this cycle of experience it passes through all the lower forms of life, but its orbit being spiral, ever ascending, it is never required to enter the same form of life a second time, never compelled to taste of the same fruit twice, never forced back into a form through which it has once passed.

Man is not, by any means, the acme of perfection, nor the climax of evolution; but contains within his form all the states through which he has already passed, and in addition, those in embryo through which his future evolution in super-mundane spheres will enable him to progress. Man is simply the point of transition from mundane to super-mundane realms of life. From mineral up to man there are seven evolutionary states of life, and from man up to the angel there are seven more. Man, therefore, stands midway between the mineral and the angel. He is ushered into physical life in the human form because he has earned the right to that form by virtue of the soul's evolutionary journey through the lower realms of impersonal being. He possesses the potencies both of mortality and of immortality; he has the possibility of becoming either God or Devil.

In man the acquired experience of attraction and repulsion, the various manifestations of the love principle as tabulated by his soul, blossom forth as Self-Consciousness. This self-consciousness is a much wider perception than is possible in any of the lower forms of existence, but it is by no means the highest state of consciousness possible even to embodied humanity. Exceptional individuals spontaneously, and others through training, have the power to place themselves so in rapport with the universe as a whole that they discern the oneness of all life and the relation of the various life-forms to the whole. This wider mental state is called Cosmic Consciousness.

And there is still a higher consciousness, called Divine Consciousness, that can be attained while the soul occupies the physical body, in which it attains rapport with the soul sphere of the ego. This soul sphere of the ego retains the records of the ego's experiences in higher than spiritual worlds. The soul by this means has access not only to the perceptions of the astral brain, but is able to utilize the almost unlimited consciousness of a well developed spiritual brain, and even tap, through its conscious rapport with the ego, information relative to still higher spheres.

The Cause of the Fall

It will now be apparent, in spite of such an interpretation by religious hierophants who wished to place and keep woman in servility, that woman was not the cause of the fall. That man fell from a state of Edenic purity into grosser conditions through yielding to temptation is a tradition held by widely disseminated peoples. Eve yielded, and partook of the Apple of the Tree of Good and Evil, because she was promised it would bestow wisdom. This apple is the fruit of incarnated experience. The soul, therefore, descended from its spiritual state to enter physical form, where it must gain its daily bread by the sweat of its brow, because it was tempted by the desire for wisdom, which could only be attained by experiences in form.

> And the Lord God said, Behold, the man is become as one of us, to know good and evil; and now, lest he put forth his hand, and take also of the tree of life, and eat, and live forever.

What is the tree of life? Immortality is life without end. Life and consciousness are only possible in association with form. Therefore, immortal life depends upon the ability of the soul to attract to itself such forms as will enable it successfully to adapt itself to its environment; for life only expresses through form so long as there is successful adaptation to the environment. Continuous adaptation to environment is continuous life. And while the life of the physical body may undoubtedly be greatly prolonged, the earth in time will reach a state when it will no longer support physical life. Man can hope for lengthy life, but not for immortality, in the flesh. He must, therefore, if self-conscious immortality is to be attained, develop the power to attract about his soul a form of the substance of the plane whither the tides of the evolutionary life wave carry him.

Nor will he tarry indefinitely in the astral; for the astral, like the physical, is subject to changes that in time will make it unfit as his abode. Ultimately, he will be swept along by forces that are as certain as is physical death, to realms above the astral, to the spiritual realm; yes, later, to regions even above this.

But if he is to survive on the spiritual plane; that is, if he is to retain consciousness, he must have the power to build himself a form of spiritual substance. Such a form can retain, as modes of motion, all the past experiences of the soul, if points of contact are provided by which the slower velocities of astral substances can transform their energy into spiritual velocities. To carry the consciousness into spiritual realms, vibratory rates must be set up of sufficient frequency that they will organize spiritual substance into a form which will receive from the astral body, and retain, the states of consciousness recorded there.

The rates of motion of common worldly thoughts, those of base desires, and those of selfish interest, have too low a frequency to influence spiritual substance. The person who has no higher thoughts and aspirations than these does not build a spiritual body. If he ever gets a spiritual body, which he probably will, he will have to organize it by noble aspirations, unselfish endeavor, and devoted love on the astral plane, after physical death.

Individual survival depends upon the ability of the entity to adapt itself to ever-changing environment. There is no such thing as rest in nature; there is an eternal procession of creation and destruction of form. Continuous consciousness, therefore, depends upon the ability continuously to adjust the internal relations to the external relations. Conscious life consists of this adjustment, and if it is to be without end, there is Immortality.

To accomplish such a progressive adaptation the soul is concerned with but two factors: Love and Wisdom. These are the tools with which it works. They are equally important and essential, and the successful performance of its task depends upon their continuous application to an increasing range of material. And in this application, quality is important as well as quantity.

The Method of Redemption

The plan of action by which Self-Conscious Immortality is to be attained is this: Man must develop, to the highest possible extent, the attributes of Love and Wisdom.

Knowledge of physical phenomena is essential on the physical plane, but life on the higher planes requires man to gather, through study, meditation, and the exercise of the psychic senses and the higher states of consciousness, as much information as possible about higher realms and about living the life of the spirit. Furthermore, in the exercise of the wisdom which contributes to immortality, the attitude toward the various events of life, the freeing them of the dross of experience, and combining them mentally so they will flux to give an intensity of vibration sufficient to affect the higher velocity of spiritual substance, is important. This subject is given detailed discussion in Course 3, *Spiritual Alchemy*.

Love, also, like wisdom, is of various grades, and man must strive for quality. He must not permit his love nature to atrophy; for upon love, fully as much as upon wisdom, depends immortality. Nor in the exercise of love should he make the mistake of trying that which psychology proves to be impossible, trying to love all without first loving one or more of the individuals embraced within the all. The love of husband and wife, of parent and child, are sacred, and are the most certain steps by which is developed the love of God, the love of mankind, and the love of all creatures.

This discussion has now shown, I trust, that the soul embraces all the various states of consciousness organized in astral substance and in spiritual substance by the monad in its descent from spirit to matter and in its evolution from mineral upward. This organization of energy which constitutes the soul results from its experiences with form.

To attain immortality the soul must have the love and wisdom to construct for itself forms in which to function on higher planes of existence than the physical and the astral. To do this it must continue to exercise and develop Love and Wisdom to a degree that it can influence the substances of such higher planes. To gain as much information about all other entities in the universe and one's proper relation to them is the exercise of the greatest Wisdom. To work persistently to be of greatest possible service in this universal society is the expression of the highest love. A life devoted to the exercise of such Wisdom and such Love builds for itself an imperishable form on the spiritual plane that provides, here and now, for Self-Conscious Immortality.

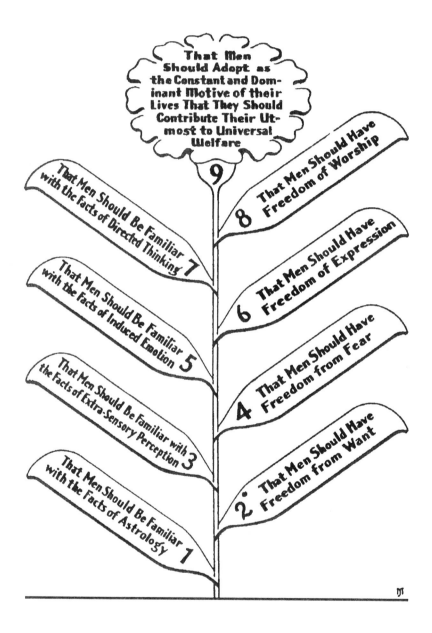

Chapter 5 _____

Physiology and Correspondence

_____

A S there is a strict correspondence between the inner and the outer, between functions exercising on one plane and functions exercising on other planes, the physiology of man may be used as an index to occult processes, and to the nature of functions exercised by man on other than physical planes. By the application of this law of correspondence we shall acquire a clearer conception, I believe, of certain principles that are of vital importance to the welfare of man.

If we are to know anything about that which remains occult we must study correspondences. That which cannot be perceived, which has no recognizable form, can only be recognized by its formative action. The form presented by any object or entity necessarily represents the sum total of the various energies that converge in it; that is, the form is the expression of the internal attributes, and there must be a strict correspondence between the internal attributes and the form. Thus, if we find certain qualities expressed in the form, we are warranted in concluding they are the manifestation of similar internal attributes, or they exist without an adequate internal cause. If the latter be possible, the nature of the real is forever a closed book, and there can be no science of occultism. As the occult can only be recognized through its influence upon form, the correspondence of the form to the energies it expresses is the only measure we possess for gauging occult forces.

The occult is that which is hidden, and it can only be apprehended by comparing it with that which is revealed. A form is always the expression of a formative principle. The outward is ever the manifestation of the inward. The visible results from the action of the invisible. The science of occultism, consequently, is based upon the fact that there is a strict correspondence between the inner and the outer, the below and the above, the effect and the cause; in other words, that the visible and known constitutes the proportional measure of the invisible and unknown.

When, therefore, we are brought in contact with such loose thinking as the assertion that a certain individual is really a man incarnated in a woman's body and that another individual is a woman incarnated in a man's body, we should cite the law of correspondences. Insomuch as the body and the actions are masculine, they must be the expression of masculine forces. In as much as the body and actions are feminine, they are the expression of a feminine nature. If female forces can express as a masculine form, or if masculine forces can express as a feminine form, we are warranted in asserting also that heat can express as cold, and that light can express as darkness. Logical thinking requires that there shall be an adequate and proportional cause for every observed effect.

The Soul Always Functions Through a Form

Now on the physical plane man has a body through which he functions. Likewise, on whatever plane of existence man may express in the future he must possess a body. The absence of form is nothingness. And as nothingness lacks expression, every existing thing must have a form. The soul of man, therefore, if it persists, must manifest through a form or body. But the body through which it manifests need not be material; it may be composed of substance of any plane or existence. It is composed of the substance of the plane on which the soul at the time manifests.

Man while still occupying a physical body is not confined in his expression exclusively to the physical plane. He manifests strongly in the electromagnetic Boundary-Line region, the astral plane is the scene of most of his unconscious activity, and in the expression of his nobler sentiments and higher ideals he also manifests upon the spiritual plane. Under normal circumstances man possesses not only a physical body, an electromagnetic body, and an astral body, but also at least the rudiments of a spiritual form.

These various bodies are replicas of each other insofar as the planes to which they belong permit. The physical body belongs to a plane of existence where velocities are so low that things have the properties which we call material. The electromagnetic body belongs to a velocity of existence where material properties give way to the peculiar ones found in light and other electromagnetic phenomena.

At this velocity, for instance, time stands still. The astral body belongs to a realm of still higher velocities in which space, time and gravitation as we know them no longer obtain, but give way to still other properties; these are explained in considerable detail in Course 4, *Ancient Masonry* and Course 9, *Mental Alchemy*. The spiritual body, furthermore, is a body on a plane where still higher velocities, and still more unbelievable properties obtain.

Yet aside from such differences as relate to the inherent qualities of the planes on which they manifest, every organ and function in the physical body is also present in the electromagnetic body, the astral body, and the spiritual body. The conditions of the spiritual plane, however, do not permit the various organs to be present in their grosser form. We should not think of the spiritual body as possessing a heart, a stomach and kidneys modeled in their shape after these organs of the physical body. But the spiritual body does have organs that perform on the spiritual plane corresponding functions. Due allowance being made for the difference in plane, there is a strict correspondence between the organs and functions of the physical body and the organs and functions of the spiritual body. Let us consider, however, those which exist between the physical body and the astral form.

The physical body is composed of protoplasm and its secretions. And in a similar manner, the astral body is composed of psychoplasm, this being the term used to designate inner-plane substance organized by thought and feeling into a definite composition suitable for inclusion in the astral form. Psychoplasm is organized of thought elements even as protoplasm is organized from the elements of matter.

The protoplasm of the physical body is organized further into definite cells, and these cells of various kinds go to build up the organs and structures of the material form. Certain types of cells build up the nervous system, other types of cells form the muscular system, still others contribute themselves to the osseous system. Some cells unite to do the work of the heart, some to perform the work of the stomach, and still others form the protective covering called the skin. And in a corresponding manner the ten families of thought-elements which each are ruled by one of the planets unite in various combinations to produce the different types of thought-cells within the astral body, and these are organized not merely to perform functions relative to each of the twelve departments of life, but in those associations with each other which enable them to do the work indicated by the aspects of the individual's astrological chart.

The oldest of all desires is the desire to survive and be something. This most powerful desire, that for significance, as explained in Chapter 5, Course 5, *Esoteric Psychology,* expresses as a positive and a negative, as the reproductive desire and the nutritive desire. Fundamental desires of all living things—plants, animals and men—are food hunger and sex hunger. These hungers being of such great importance upon the physical plane, we may well inquire as to their existence upon the inner planes of life. The functions of physical life by which these two basic yearnings are satisfied must, by the law of correspondence, represent all-important functions in the life of spiritual man.

Food Hunger

We are aware that the body is unable to survive unless it is supplied with food. Action of any kind consumes energy, and this energy must be replenished if action is to continue. Food in its various forms constitutes the energy supply that permits the continuation of activity. This activity may be that of internal changes, or that of movements of the body or of its organs; but wherever life expresses there is movement of some kind that consumes energy. All forms of life, therefore, must have food. Bacteria have various sources of food. The chief food supply of plants is the carbon of the atmosphere. The food supply of animals consists of plants, or other animals, of water, and of the oxygen of the air. Nothing upon the earth lives without food; nor have we any reason to suppose that on the spiritual plane, or even on higher planes, life without food is possible.

Of course, the nature of the food changes with the plane of activity, just as the nature of the food for various forms of life is different. To sustain the electromagnetic form and afford energy for objective thought, as explained in detail in Chapter 9, Course 5, *Esoteric Psychology,* man acquires in his food protein molecules which contain the high-frequency energy of the lightning which fixed the nitrogen which plant life took from the soil. And to feed the upper-octave electromagnetic Boundary-Line energies required for direction and proper control of inner-plane activities, the electrical energies of the nervous system must be released in unusual volume and high-frequency, as explained in full detail in 5th Award NOT SOLD Manuscript, Breathing to Acquire Adequate Electrification.

In order that it may survive and continue active, not only the electromagnetic body but also the astral form must be supplied with energy. This is the law on all planes; that whatever energy is used must have a source of supply. And while planetary radiations afford a certain amount of the energy used by the thought-cells and thought structures of the astral body, and during physical life the astral counterpart of the food partaken of and assimilated affords some, the thoughts of the individual provide by far the most important supply. Or to express it still another way, the most valuable food supply of the astral body, not merely of man but of all other life forms, is that derived from experience.

Every experience contributes energy to the astral form. States of consciousness cause the astral body to extract nourishment from the astral region surrounding it, much as sunlight causes a green leaf to extract nourishment from the atmosphere. The light of the sun is responsible for plant nourishment, and the light of consciousness is responsible for the nourishment of the astral body. Whenever there is a ray of consciousness, whenever there is a mood, a feeling, a thought, or an aspiration, the astral body receives nourishment.

This food of the astral body may be wholesome, or it may be the reverse. If the factors composing it are associated with the feeling of pleasure they form constructive compounds in the astral body. These in turn work to attract fortunate events into the life. If the factors partaken of are associated with the feeling of displeasure or pain, they form destructive compounds. In this case they work from the inner plane to attract unfortunate events into the life. Course 9, *Mental Alchemy*, is largely devoted to explaining about such astral foods, and how to select those which when assimilated will enable the individual to have the kind of life and destiny he desires.

The spiritual body, the body that the soul after it leaves the astral plane must function in if it is to survive, also must have its food. The laws of nature are not transcended on the spiritual plane. Movement and accomplishment on the spiritual plane consume energy, and this energy must be derived from some previously existing source. If man is to have a spiritual body in which to function on the spiritual plane, he must supply it with the food necessary to its growth; and if the spiritual body, once grown, is to continue active, more food must be supplied to it. Life on any plane of existence implies the capture, storage and expenditure of energy. The source of this energy is called food. To grow to maturity and perform its functions the spiritual body must be supplied with spiritual food.

The food of the spiritual body is provided by certain grades of thought that combine to produce high vibratory rates, and by certain moods and emotional states that in themselves are of exceptionally high-frequency vibratory rates. Course 3, *Spiritual Alchemy*, is devoted to explaining how to develop thought-food of the quality necessary to build a vigorous spiritual form, but it will not be out of place here to indicate the general principle involved.

The spiritual body is the substance of a different plane than the astral; or to state it differently, its velocities belong to a different phase of existence. To illustrate: A bar of iron normally has those velocities which we associate with physical substance. But suppose we heat it. The molecules increase their vibrations and communicate their energy to surrounding molecules, so that whatever touches the bar also becomes hot. This heat energy of the bar, while it may be used as a source of power to perform work on the physical plane, does not affect appreciably energies which have a velocity which gives them other than physical properties.

But if the bar is heated to high enough temperature, if its molecular and therefore physical vibrations become of sufficient frequency, they impart energy to the Boundary-Line region. The bar becomes red hot and electromagnetic energies called radiant heat and light come into existence which have a velocity greater than things of the physical world, and possess properties which physical things do not. At the velocity of these electromagnetic energies particles gain tremendously in mass, shrink amazingly in length in the direction of their travel, and time stands still.

Even as the cold bar fails thus to affect electromagnetic Boundary-Line energies, so the ordinary energies of the astral body and of animal-like thinking fail to generate velocities sufficiently high to affect the spiritual body, or to afford it nourishment. It is only thoughts in special combinations, and especially those with vibratory rates entirely above self-interest, that furnish the energy which enables the spiritual body to indraw spiritual substance. This energy derived from the motive, Contribute Your Utmost to Universal Welfare, builds a complex and highly organized spiritual form.

Sex Hunger

Now let us turn from food hunger to sex hunger as the other pole of the one irrepressible biological urge for significance: As man's stronger emotions are more commonly associated with the expression of his love life, it is obvious that this love life, in its various manifestations, constitutes one of the most important supplies of food for the astral body. The astral food thus derived may be intensely harmonious and act powerfully in the construction of beneficial compounds, or it may be disastrously discordant and thus act powerfully in the construction of misfortune-attracting compounds. Furthermore, as the quality of love's expression varies from gross bestiality up to ineffable sublimity, the quality of the astral food derived from expression of the love nature may be anything from fetid corruption to spiritual ambrosia. It is thus possible to elevate love to a plane of expression that is entirely above the physical; the expression being spiritual, and consequently furnishing strength and nutriment directly to the spiritual body. But as this phase of the love life is discussed in detail in Course 4, *Ancient Masonry*, we will here take up another phase, which considers union, not from the standpoint of the emotional energies, but from the standpoint of energy exchange.

Sexual union throughout nature's various life forms is not merely for the purpose of reproduction. In fact, reproduction seems to be a secondary object. Reproduction takes place in innumerable life-forms without sexual union. The aphis, insects which are so great a nuisance to plant growers, reproduce independent of sexual union. There are plants that reproduce without union of male and female parts, in addition to those that reproduce by means of runners, those that stool out, and those that grow from shoots, cuttings, and tubers. The object of sexual union is not to make reproduction possible, but through an exchange of qualities to give the offspring, if offspring is the result, attributes not possessed by one of the parents independent of the other.

Some of the protozoa, low forms of animal life, reproduce themselves repeatedly without union with another protozoan. But unless they unite with another protozoan after a certain length of time they die. If they do find and mate with another, they continue to reproduce by subdivision, and do not die. Union is not necessary for reproduction, but it is necessary for continued life.

In the sexual union of these low forms of animal life there is a complete fusion of protoplasm and chromosomes. When they separate it is believed that each has exchanged some of its substance for some of the substance of the other. Both are different in composition than before, and both have new vitality. When they subdivide in the production of offspring, the offspring may partake, not merely of the qualities of one, but of the qualities of both.

In all reproductive cells, either of plants or animals, there are minute filaments, called chromosomes. The number of chromosomes in the reproductive cell is constant for each species of animal. These chromosomes, with genes strung along them like beads, are the physical carriers of hereditary traits. Half the chromosomes of the fertilized cell are furnished by the male, and half by the female. The plant or animal, then, that grows from a fertilized seed, may contain the potentialities of the ancestors on both sides of the family. Only a portion of these potentialities express, however, in any individual. The laws governing this are set forth in Chapter 4, Course 17, *Cosmic Alchemy*. Here it is sufficient to say in this connection that because the offspring contains genes from both parents it may differ widely from either parent through the combination of these hereditary factors. This gives rise to variation and makes evolution possible.

The union of male and female entities is for the purpose of exchanging qualities. But we need not confine our observations entirely to the physical plane. Instead of directing our attention to plants and lower animals, let us consider human relations, not merely physical relations, but all those relations involving electromagnetic exchange.

When we clasp the hand of another in token of welcome or friendship there usually passes from the body of each to the other electrical energy. Each has partaken of energy that previously belonged to the other. In such casual relations no great quantities of energy are exchanged. But in the more intimate relations of life there may be such a complete exchange of electromagnetic energy through the blending of the electromagnetic bodies that each noticeably partakes of the characteristics of the other. It is a common observation that people who live long together grow to look alike and act alike. The exchange of energies is so complete that each loses part of his individuality in the other.

Such exchanges of electrical energies either in marriage or in less intimate association may be very beneficial, or it may be very harmful, depending upon the natural harmony between the individuals, and upon the quality of energy exchanged. But for a proper balance of the electromagnetic forces some contact with the opposite sex seems essential. Men who go to far regions where they see no women for a long time, and both men and women who are confined where they do not meet the opposite sex, exhibit a strange irritability. But there may be an unconscious exchange of electromagnetic energies, and marked benefit therefrom, without close physical contact. Merely to be in the same room with others, or to engage in conversation with them, offers opportunities for sufficient exchange to overcome magnetic tensions and to re-establish nervous balance.

Whenever people meet there is likewise an exchange of astral energies. Thoughts originating in different minds may fuse and blend to form an entirely new idea. Among people closely associated, particularly in the marriage relation, there is also a very complete exchange of astral energies, each influencing the thoughts and feelings of the other. Unconsciously, by their thoughts, people continually give mental treatments to their acquaintances. If they think and express kind thoughts concerning an acquaintance, these energies tend to enter the astral body of the acquaintance as constructive elements. If the thoughts are critical and abusive they tend to enter the astral body as destructive elements. In associating with one another, in exchanging ideas, in thinking about each other although far separated on the physical plane, we are exchanging astral energies. Through these exchanges of astral energies we are not what we were before.

We receive mental elements, both pernicious and beneficial, from others, and they receive from us. When we are no longer capable of both giving and receiving ideas, of exchanging mental energies, we are mentally dead. When we can no longer learn from others we have ceased to progress. It is only through mental exchanges that the mind is rejuvenated, only through the exchange of astral energies that mental vigor is maintained. If our minds are to remain young we must find opportunity periodically for association that will permit a complete exchange of ideas.

Union On the Spiritual Plane

Better to understand this function of union, especially as applied to the spiritual plane, it now seems advisable to trace the steps by which sperm and germ enter into union for the purpose of producing a new individual. As we are discussing human life and its possibilities, although the process is very much the same in all plants and animals, it seems better for the purpose of drawing close correspondences to use as example the human seed.

Both the ovule and the spermatazoon before they are capable of entering into union which forms the nucleus of a new human body

must undergo quite a complicated preliminary process. These changes by which they are ripened for a final fusion into a single organism
are called maturation. Maturation of the seed is marked by three
chief stages: In the first stage the seed is of full size, but not yet
capable of permanent union with another cell of the opposite sex.
From this stage it arrives at the second and third stages by two
successive cell divisions that differ somewhat from ordinary cell
division.

Now in the cells of each species of animal there is a characteristic
number of filaments called chromosomes. These chromosomes, as I
have already mentioned, are the physical carriers of heredity, and
the typical number for the tissue cells of man is forty-eight. But in
the ripening of the seed, just previous to the first cell division, there
is a pairing of the chromosomes, it being believed that one of each
pair, that thus fuse to become one, was originally paternal in origin,
and the other was maternal in origin. By the marriage of the
chromosomes they are reduced in number to twenty-four. The fusion
of paternal and maternal chromosomes corresponds to the fusion of
selfish and unselfish desires in man under the influence of true
wisdom.

Following this internal reduction occurs the first of the two
processes of cell division. In the case of the ovule, one of the two
ovules thus produced, each containing twenty-four chromosomes,
is of less size than the other. It is called the first polar body, and is
cast off as of no further value. So also man in the development of his
soul learns to free himself from the physical body and function
consciously in the astral form. The extrusion of the first polar body,
then, corresponds to the elimination of bondage to the physical
plane.

The first polar body, after being cast aside, may again divide in
the formation of two cells, both of which later disintegrate. Thus in
leaving his physical body to travel in the astral, or in leaving it at
death, man must also abandon his electromagnetic body, which is
closely associated with the physical form. Both the electromagnetic
body and the physical body are left behind when the soul functions
consciously on the astral plane.

In the third state of ripening, cell division again takes place, with
an equal splitting of the chromosomes, so that in each resulting cell
there are twenty-four chromosomes. In this division, likewise, one
portion is much smaller in size than the other. It is known as the
second polar body, and is cast off to disintegrate. This extrusion of

the second polar body corresponds to man freeing himself from his astral body as well as from the physical form. It corresponds to his state when he is able to function consciously in his spiritual form.

Until these two polar bodies are cast off the egg is not ripe, and is unprepared for fertile union. And so long as man is chained by his physical senses and subject to astral intoxication he will attempt in vain to find his true spiritual mate. The union of twin souls, the marriage of the Lamb, is a spiritual union, successfully accomplished only after both have ripened to spiritual maturity.

The chromosomes of the seed may be compared to the various desires that determine the character of a man and give direction to his activities. Before he undertakes spiritual training these desires are rather equally divided between those purely selfish and those more or less unselfish. But as soon as he perceives the truth, that his own advancement and welfare are bound up with the advancement and welfare of all others, that so-called unselfish actions are those from which ultimately he receives greatest benefit, and that all so-called selfish actions always ultimately are detrimental to his welfare, these two sets of desires, the selfish and the unselfish, like the maternal and paternal chromosomes of the maturing seed, amalgamate. Selfish and unselfish desires unite in the formation of desires based upon the motive, Contribute Your Utmost to Universal Welfare.

After physical death man functions in his astral body, leaving the physical form behind. When traveling in the astral, while still possessing a physical body, he also leaves the physical form behind. To function on the spiritual plane he must not only discard the physical body and the electromagnetic body—corresponding to the first polar body which when cast off again divides—but he must leave his astral body—corresponding to the second polar body—also behind. At the second death man permanently loses his astral form, and henceforth must function in a spiritual body.

Now in order for the seed to grow into human form it is absolutely essential not only that there shall be a reduction of the chromosomes by fusion, and the two successive stages of cell division described, but that the female seed must meet and fuse into a single form with a male seed. Without the permanent blending in a single form of ovum and spermatazoon the seed never grows into a child. Likewise, according to the Ancient Hermetic Teachings, the angelic form is only developed from the permanent fusion of a male and a female soul.

This doctrine, handed down from the remote past, deals with a condition commonly attained only after the death of the physical body and also after the second death, or disintegration of the astral body. Before this permanent spiritual union of twin souls can take place it is absolutely necessary that each shall have developed a well organized spiritual body. Before this marriage of the Lamb, unselfish and selfish desires must be wed in true wisdom, there must be freedom from physical limitations, and freedom from astral enthrall-ment. It has nothing to do with physical marriage, and nothing to do with astral fusions. It is the final union, on the boundary of the sixth and seventh state of the spiritual world, of the spiritual bodies of a male and a female soul.

The Nine-Point Plan Which Must Be Followed

The mere union in the spiritual world of a male and a female soul, however, does not provide the form and functions of an angel, nor does the mere union of spermatazoon and ovum insure that a child will be born. No more so than that the union of inner-plane facts and outer-plane facts, such as are represented by the two wavy lines which symbolize the sign Aquarius, alone insure there will be the New Civilization which the humanitarian side of the sign demands of the Aquarian Age. In each case, if that of which the union is but the start is properly to develop and result in the promised birth of something more perfect and glorious, development must take place which follows a definite nine-point plan. And even as in numerals the number 10 starts a new cycle, so the tenth step, of course, is the one of transition which marks the birth of that which has undergone the nine phases of gestation.

While the nine-point plan and its final result on each level very broadly correspond to the chain of ten planets, much more detail can be learned from the precise correspondence of the planet or sign to the sequence number in the plan. This astrological rulership of the numerals is set forth in Course 6, *The Sacred Tarot*.

In the Cycle of Necessity the soul undergoes development in nine realms before becoming the transcendent angel which permits its birth into the celestial realm from which it started. This is the nine-point plan which to be successful it must follow: I Celestial, II Spiritual, III Astral, IV Mineral, V Vegetable, VI Animal, VII Human, VIII Astral, IX Spiritual. With these nine phases of gestation completed, Self-Conscious immortality has been won and transition may take place in the perfect angelic form to X Celestial.

In the adjustment of mankind to the Aquarian Age, now at hand, the tenth and final step is the attainment of a truly enlightened and humanitarian civilization. And to make this transition properly, humanity must proceed according to the nine-point plan which follows:

As a cooperative intelligence working for the realization of God's Great Evolutionary Plan, the development of the powers and possibilities of his own soul is of paramount importance to the individual, and of paramount importance to the whole in proportion as the abilities and characteristics thus developed contribute to universal welfare. And this character development is influenced and conditioned by the environmental forces which it contacts not merely on one plane, but on both the inner and the outer plane.

Both the behavior of the individual and the events which come into his life are primarily determined by the desires of the thought-cells and thought structures of his own soul. These thought-cell desires, in turn are determined by the experiences which have formed them or added to them; experiences with both the inner-plane environment and the outer-plane environment. Secondarily, the behavior of the individual and the events which come into his life are determined by planetary or other inner-plane energies added to the thought-cells of his soul at a given time, which increase their activity and modify somewhat their desires, and by the facilities afforded by the outer-plane environment to some actions and events and the resistance the outer-plane environment offers to others.

Either freedom from want or any one of the other three essential freedoms which should be present in the outer-plane environment, implies effective use of abilities on materials, and the avoidance of disaster. Square pegs in round holes, people engaged in enterprises for which they have no talent, and people engaging in enterprises at times when failure is sure to result, do not lead to freedom from want. Effectively to guide character development, and to have freedom from want in ample measure, as well as to have the other essential freedoms, the 9-point plan states:

FIRST, that men should be familiar with the Facts of Astrology.

A lifelong physical environment of illiteracy, poverty, disease and heartrending toil, such as vast portions of the world have experienced, is not conducive to developing the potentialities of the soul. Nor is the acceptance of the doctrines of atheistic materialism.

Under such physical environmental handicaps the individual ig-
nores or denies the existence of his soul, and is trained to function,
whether his intellect is active or numbed by hardships, only on the
self-seeking plane of the brutes.

To have sufficient leisure from incessant toil, and to possess the
things properly to live, while thought is given to the soul, and effort
spent in character development, the 9-point plan states:

SECOND, that men should have Freedom from Want.

A haphazard universe moving without purpose gives few assuran-
ces that the individual will not be overwhelmed by disaster. Atheistic
materialism, by force of arms if able to do so, and by cunning
suppression of all facts which prove there are inner-plane forces, or
life on any plane but the physical, if force of arms does not give it
world dominance, is determined to compel all men to accept such a
purposeless universe, in which selfish force and brutal shrewdness
are extolled as the highest virtues. But millions of people, past and
present, through their own personal experiences have proven to
themselves that there is a Supreme Guiding Intelligence permeating
the universe which, under special conditions, men can contact. And
millions of people, past and present, through their own personal
experiences have proven to themselves that physical death does not
end either consciousness or the progress of personality. And in order
that people may thus prove to themselves the existence of God, and
the persistence of life and personality after the dissolution of the
physical, the 9-point plan states:

*THIRD, that men should be familiar with the Facts of Extra Sensory
Perception.*

There is possible either a constructive or a destructive approach to
every situation of life. An approach which is accompanied by the
emotion of fear is to that extent destructive, for fear is an agent of
ineffectiveness and the foe of health and happiness. Even the facts
of astrology when viewed from the standpoint of fear may be made
detrimental, and freedom from want in proper measure is repelled
by fear. Yet the attitude of fear is a conditioned state. It arises from
considering the possibility or probability of want, disease, or other
disagreeable things, including the cessation of life. Confidence that
disagreeable things will not happen, that dangers can be sur-
mounted, and that death merely brings a continuation of life on
another plane, assist in conditioning the emotions to resist this most

destructive of all attitudes. In order to promote happiness, usefulness and spirituality, the 9-point plan states:

FOURTH, that men should have Freedom from Fear.

The success with which an individual is able to express his natural aptitudes, to contribute to the welfare of all, and to develop his own soul depends, in addition to his familiarity with astrology and ESP and possession of the four freedoms, on the desires of the thought-cells and thought structures of his own soul. The conditions of external environment afforded by the four freedoms facilitate soul growth, and knowledge of astrology and ESP indicate the best course to pursue. But, in spite of knowledge and environment, both the actions which take place which we call behavior, and the events which come into the life, are chiefly determined by the way the thought-cells and thought structures within the soul then feel.

The thought-cells and thought structures have the desires they do, and therefore influence the behavior and events in the manner they do, because of the feeling energy and the emotional energy which have been built into them in the past. And the only way to get them to have different desires, and consequently influence the behavior in a more beneficial manner, and to work from the inner plane to attract more favorable events, is to impart to them appropriate feeling and emotion. To do this intelligently requires the use of deliberately induced emotion. Thus the 9-point plan states:

FIFTH, that men should be familiar with the Facts of Induced Emotion.

But men will not be permitted to become familiar with the facts of astrology or the facts of ESP if atheistic materialism is able to gain the intellectual dictatorship over the people of the world it desires. Nor will it be possible to have either freedom from want or freedom from fear if such intellectual dictatorship is permitted to suppress facts relative to economic conditions and political oppression. To gain power through which to use others for their own selfish and brutal ends, tyrants always have found it essential to suppress and distort the facts.

But even when they have free access to facts, men also have individual aptitudes without the expression of which, either in the vocation or the avocation, they are unable to find happiness and are unable to contribute most to universal welfare. These creative talents should not be wasted through denying them opportunity for exercise. Therefore the 9-point plan states:

SIXTH, that men should have Freedom of Expression.

The proper exercise of each of the four freedoms, and the proper employment of the facts of astrology, the facts of ESP and the facts of induced emotion, that these may Contribute Their Utmost to Universal Welfare, imply that intelligence must be applied to formulate an effective plan, and that the energies instead of being permitted to wander aimlessly from this plan, be directed into its fulfillment. The energies tend to flow into and develop whatever thought the mind consistently entertains. Thought ever affords, both on the outer plane and the inner plane, the pattern of action. Consequently the 9-point plan states:

SEVENTH, that men should be familiar with the Facts of Directed Thinking.

The most important thing in the universe is God's Great Evolutionary Plan. The conception of this plan depends upon the spiritual and intellectual level of the individual trying to comprehend it. Also, as physical science and spiritual science discover new facts any adequate conception of this plan must be enlarged to embrace them.

To the individual, the most important thing of all is the progress of his own soul. And soul progression cannot be applied to him from the outside by others, no more than can intelligence. It requires effort on his own part to live, not as someone else believes, but according to his own highest conception at the time. It requires the liberty, as more complete information is gained, to modify the conduct to conform to this new information. Therefore the 9-point plan states:

EIGHTH, that men should have Freedom of Worship.

Both the progress of his own soul and the unfoldment of God's Great Evolutionary Plan depend upon the welfare of the various individuals who make up the conscious cells embraced within the whole. What affects one individual, in some degree affects all individuals. The 9-point plan therefore states:

NINTH, that men should adopt as the constant and dominant motives of their lives that they should contribute their Utmost to Universal Welfare.

The four freedoms set forth in association with the negative, or even, numbers, 2, 4, 6, and 8, relate largely to important factors of the outer-plane environment. There is no assumption that we know all we should about them. In fact, as evolution advances, we are sure to learn details which will assist us more perfectly to realize these four freedoms. And we should strive persistently to acquire such knowledge, which, no doubt, will be made available through the ordinary channels of education.

The four orders of facts set forth in association with the positive, or odd, numbers, 1,3,5, and 7, however, relate largely to important factors of the inner-plane environment. As information relating to them is mostly lacking through the more ordinary channels of education, the Brotherhood of Light lessons were written to make it accessible to all.

Yet these lessons, which are as comprehensive as it is possible to make them at this day, make no assumption that we know all we should about these four orders of inner-plane activities. In fact, although we now know the fundamental principles through which each operates, as times goes on we are sure to gain many new details which will assist us more perfectly to utilize these four different categories of inner-plane forces. As this new knowledge is gained it will be included in revised copies of The Brotherhood of Light lessons. And to hasten acquiring it, The Church of Light maintains three active research departments: The Brotherhood of Light Astrological Research Department, the ESP Research Department, and the Control of Life Research Department.

Even as Aquarius is symbolized by two wavy lines, one above the other, are there four essential freedoms which relate chiefly to the physical environment, and four orders of facts which relate chiefly to the inner-plane environment, the utilization of which are essential. But between the four outer-plane freedoms and the four inner-plane orders of facts, must ever remain as the central theme the all-inclusive principle indicated by the Deific number 9, the number of Aquarius: the constant and dominant motive in men's lives must be to Contribute Their Utmost to Universal Welfare. This is the most important factor of all in the Nine-Point Plan for the New Civilization.

The nine-point plan by which the united spermatazoon and ovum successfully develop to the point where a healthy child may be born is as follows:

During the first month the two cells that fused into one at conception undergo a constant geometrical progression of cell division so that within twenty-four hours there are thousands of cells. This process is accelerated from day to day until by the fourteenth day there is a distinct embryo, and by the end of the month the embryo is about one inch in length and the principle organs are discernible.

The second month brings remarkable increase in the size of the head, the tail becomes less conspicuous, there is rapid growth of the limbs, and the human form is definitely established.

The third month is marked by establishment of the generative organs; the limbs take definite shape and the nails form.

In the fourth month the chin, index of determination, begins to be prominent, the sex becomes well marked, and the embryo begins to show signs of life.

During the fifth month the skin becomes more consistent, and the hair is more extensively developed than previously.

In the sixth month the eye-lashes and eye-brows make their appearance, and the sternum becomes well developed.

Then comes the seventh month at the end of which if the child is born it usually lives. The bones forming the skull become strongly convex, and the central point of each, from which ossification commences, forms a noticeable prominence.

During the eighth month the most important changes are those relating to nerve force and the electromagnetic body.

The ninth month brings the final adjustment between the astral body of the child and the vibrations of the planets. This period is not at an end until the astrological rates correspond closely, both in trend and in harmony or discord, with the thought-cell pattern of the unborn child.

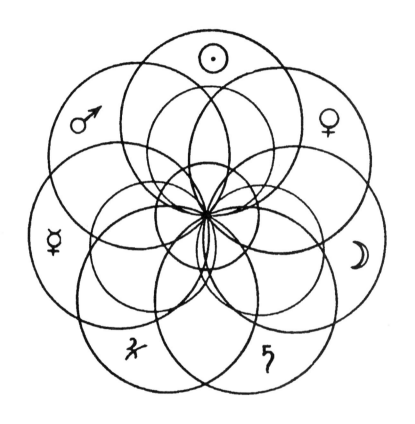

Chapter 6

The Doctrine of Signatures

T HE English word signature is derived from the Latin "signare," meaning to sign. A signature, therefore, is a mark of identification. The Latin "docere," from which the word doctrine is derived, signifies to teach. In occult science "The Doctrine of Signatures" relates to that which is taught about the marks placed upon all things by stellar influences. It is of these stellar marks of identification that I shall have considerable to say.

Turning for the moment from the stars, we find that the owner of livestock places a brand upon his cattle by which his property may be recognized. The manufacturer, that its source may be recognized, stamps a trademark upon his product. The public official places his seal upon legal documents to denote their importance and character; and correspondents sign their letters with their autographs that no doubt may arise in the mind of the recipient as to whom the sender may be. These are circumstances commonly recognized. But less commonly recognized is the fact that all things external have upon them the stamp of their origin in the cause world and that this relates them as definite kin to certain other things.

It is not surprising that one may fail to recognize the seal of the Emperor of China or the signature of an Indian prince. Yet to one familiar with the language, history, and customs of China and India such signs are evidence enough upon which to establish the source of a missive and determine the prestige of its sender. Likewise, the man in the street is ignorant of the signs by which the planets and zodiacal signs mark their progeny; but those familiar with celestial language recognize these marks and, in addition to deducing their common origin, quickly perceive the relationship of anything so sealed with other objects bearing the same impress.

Now to facilitate the study of the Doctrine of Signatures let us turn to that much misunderstood tradition the Jewish Kabala. Not that the Jews knew more about occult doctrine than other ancient peoples, perhaps much less than some; but because through their contact with the priesthood of both Egypt and Chaldea they became familiar with the Mysteries that in these countries were taught only to initiates. Moses, the great law giver of the Jews, according to the most authentic tradition, was saved from the waters of the Nile by Thergmuthus, the daughter of Pharaoh Amenophis. He was raised by the Magi, or Ancient Masons, and drew from their secret teachings the religious, political, and social ideas which were the basis of the legislation of the Hebrews after their exodus from Egypt. That Moses received initiation from the Egyptian Priesthood is made apparent in the Bible, Acts 7:22 "And Moses was learned in all the wisdom of the Egyptians, and was mighty in words and in deeds." Thus did the laws and rites of Ancient Masonry pass in great measure into the theocracy which Moses founded.

The religious laws of antiquity in general and of Egypt and Chaldea in particular forbade that any part of the Mysteries should be committed to writing. These things, nevertheless, were evidently revealed by Moses to the Hebrew Elders and handed down by them until the second destruction of the Temple, because at that time it was placed in writing as the Kabala. A great deal of this traditional wisdom was also, from time to time before the advent of the written Kabala, but during and subsequent to the Babylonian captivity, concealed in the Bible. In these two Jewish books, the Bible and the Kabala, that all may read who can penetrate the veil, we have the esoteric doctrine of Chaldea and Egypt.

The Kabala describes creation as having been accomplished by means of ten emanations. Earlier than this all was without form and void.

Before proceeding with this Kabalistical explanation it is advisable to explain that universally considered there is but One Principle, but One Law, but One Truth, and but One Agent. This thought is expressed beautifully by the four-fold sphinx. It has the paws of a lion, symbolizing the One Principle—energy; the wings of an eagle expressing the One Law—sex; the body of a bull signifying the One Agent—form; and the head of a man typifying the One Truth—reality.

The Kabalists called the state prior to creation Ain Soph Aur, meaning the limitless light. It represents a condition when nothing existed but the all pervading nonatomic spirit, potential but unmanifest.

Then comes emanation, creation. The first of these
Kether, or Crown. It is merely motion, vibration. Coinc.
a partnership is formed. The nonatomic, diffusive spirit is ɾ
into more active portions and less active portions. These are rea.
to each other as positive and negative. Deity is no longer
homogeneous, but has become male and female. Here we have the
godhead of the kabalists, similar to the godhead of the world's most
popular religions. The kabala calls it Kether, Chocmah, and Binah,
rendered Crown, Wisdom, and Love, or in terms of Hermetic
philosophy, Life, Light, and Love—the God Who is a trinity, yet is
one.

This triune godhead, according to the ancient teaching, is the
spiritual sun of the universe from which flows the so-called solar ray.
The latter contains within it the potency of all that is, all that has been,
and all that ever possibly can be. It is not to be confused with the rays
of the physical sun, for it is spiritual and mental as well as physical.
The more slowly moving portions of this ray, the negative portions,
interact with one another to produce the grosser forms of substance
such as the ether of space that cushions the sun and planets and those
still less active forms with which we are more familiar as matter. The
more active moving portions of the ray, the more active portions of
this universal energy, we term spirit. This positive, finer, more subtle
energy inheres in matter of every grade and order as the instigator
of life and motion.

From the first trinity of the Sephiroth, known to western students
as Life, Light, and Love, are evolved seven more specialized emanations which constitute the Seven Active Principles of Nature. This is
brought about through the Solar Ray being refracted from seven
sub-centers around the spiritual sun. These form the seven states of
angelic life from which issue all the life-entities of our universe. Each
of these seven states corresponds to one of the seven planets. The
kabalists hold that each is presided over by an archangel, or as
modern astrologers state, each represents a family of planetary life.
Thus the planetary family corresponding to the Sun is said to be
ruled over by the archangel Michael, that corresponding to Mercury
by Raphael, that corresponding to Venus by Anael, that corresponding to the Moon by Gabriel, that corresponding to Saturn by Cassiel,
that corresponding to Jupiter by Zachariel, and the family corresponding to Mars by Samael.

Now the spiritual potencies that constitute the egos of all things
never were created, never had a beginning, never can be destroyed.

The law of conservation of energy forbids such beginning and such destruction. But they did have a point of differentiation from which they departed on their present cyclic journey, and this point of departure was within the spiritual vortex of one of the planetary families. Each ego, therefore, partakes of the attributes of one of the seven planetary families, and this may be said to constitute the character of its genius. That is, the internal nature, or individuality, of each human being corresponds to one of the planets, and this correspondence is never entirely effaced during the whole stretch of time that constitutes the soul's cycle of experience.

The two souls which embrace all the states of consciousness of the ego, partake of the planetary quality of the ego. Not only so, but they carry with them the impress of their birth-place, or environment in which differentiation took place. Thus the universe is divided into four states of life—fire, air, water, and earth—and each soul proceeds from one of these four states which are represented by the fiery, airy, watery, and earthy signs of the zodiac. It is this affinity for a certain state of life that shapes the general trend of the soul's impulses.

Furthermore, each state of life has three degrees of emanation. Thus Aries constitutes the first, Leo the second, and Sagittarius the third degree of emanation of the fiery state of life. Gemini is the first, Libra the second, and Aquarius the third degree of emanation of the airy state of life. Cancer is the first, Scorpio the second, and Pisces the third degree of emanation of the watery state of life. Taurus is the first, Virgo the second, and Capricorn the third degree of emanation of the earthy state of life. Each soul, therefore, by reason of the environment in which the differentiation of the ego occurred, also may be said to belong to a certain degree of emanation.

The motives and impulses of a soul belonging to the fiery state of life are found to be shaped largely by inspiration and enthusiasm; those belonging to the airy state of life by intellect and aspiration; those belonging to the watery state of life by sensation and emotion; and those belonging to the earthy state of life by application and practicality. If, at the same time a soul belongs to the first degree of emanation he will act from his own feelings, ideas, and inward yearnings; if he belongs to the second degree of emanation he will act to a greater extent from the motive of what other people think and advise; and if he belongs to the third degree of emanation his acts will be very largely determined by the ideas and admonitions received from others.

It is now apparent that the doctrine of signatures revolves around three chief factors which are termed Character of Genius, State of Life, and Degree of Emanation. Much as we indicate the parentage of a man by saying he belongs to Bourbon stock, so we may designate the lineage of a soul by saying it belongs to the planetary family of Mars. As we indicate the country of a man's birth by saying he was born in England, so we may indicate the broad environment of a soul's origin by saying he belongs to the Fiery state. And as the city of a person's birth might be London, so the more local environment of a soul's origin might be the First Degree of Emanation. London is in England, and the First Degree of Emanation of the Fiery State is Aries. By the use of such terms we are able to designate the parentage and birth-place of a soul just as we are able by other more familiar terms to designate a person's physical parentage and place of birth.

When accurately determined the ancestry and place of birth of an individual gives considerable information as to what may be expected of him. Likewise the planetary family and celestial environment of a soul's origin is some index to its abilities and possibilities. That is, while not complete data upon which to predict the actions of an individual or a soul, they have a real value as determining factors.

They are not complete data because after birth each individual and each soul undergoes a series of experiences. These greatly modify the qualities with which the individual or the soul is born. Subsequent environment is constantly changing the character, constantly adding new factors, constantly giving new viewpoints. Yet an Englishman born in London will not react to the same set of experiences in the same way that a North American Indian reacts to them. They will not modify the character in the same way, nor will the same viewpoint be developed from them. Ancestry and birth environment are not all to be considered in reference to character. Neither are later environment and experience to be considered all. Both the later environment and the ancestry together with the birth environment must be considered. The birth chart reveals the result of the interaction of both these factors up to the time the soul is born in human form. The Doctrine of Signatures, therefore, considers the influence of ancestry, birth environment, and subsequent experiences upon the soul, as revealed by the birth chart, and as indicating both Character and Fortune.

After its differentiation the soul-monad in its cyclic journey passes through innumerable states and phases of existence, adding new characteristics and qualities, as a traveler acquires new customs and idioms of speech without effacing the marks of birth-place and parentage. One traveler, however, is attracted to certain customs while being repelled by usages that are attractive to other travelers. Likewise each soul on its long journey is attracted more strongly to certain forms of life, and finds more complete expression through them, while souls of different origin are attracted strongly to, and find more complete expression through, other life forms. The soul belonging to the planetary family of Mars, for instance, whenever it finds itself in a Saturnine environment expresses itself only with greatest difficulty, and the Venusian soul feels little affinity for the regal surroundings and majestic qualities of the sun.

The soul is a traveler, and as such is ever collecting and disbursing. Its baggage at any given time represents its original equipment and its collections, minus its disbursements. That is, the soul in its journey constantly attracts and repulses forms. By virtue of its original polarity it shuns some things and embraces others, the sum total of its experiences and original equipment constituting the quality of the soul at any given point in its journey.

It may be, and often is, so surrounded by baggage attracted enroute that it is difficult to perceive its original characteristics, but these nonetheless exist. Such inherent attributes by which we recognize its degree of emanation, its state of life, and the character of its genius, in other words its attractive and repulsive power, we may call its original signature.

The Doctrine of Signatures, however, is not confined to entities; for species, genera, races, families, kingdoms, all have group signatures. This means that the members of a group all vibrate in some particular respect to a common vibratory rate or its multiple. They are sympathetically united to, and thus said to be ruled by, the energies of some planet or zodiacal sign. In this circumstance we find the greatest practical application of the Doctrine.

Yet when we are informed that peppers, mustard, nettle, thistle, onions, and horseradish are plants ruled by the sign Aries we are not to conclude that the individual entities of all onions, peppers, etc., had their origin in the fiery state of life, first degree of emanation; for the individual entities may have had widely varied origins in the celestial spaces. Some may have sprung from each of the several states, degrees, and families; for in its pilgrimage from mineral to man the entity traverses the whole ascending scale of life. The soul that now occupies the regal body of man was once incarnated in each of the progressive steps—some allowance being made for different requirements—from the lowly crystal atom through the various evolutionary forms up to his now exalted state. He has in turn occupied species ruled by all the various families, states, and degrees of emanation.

What is meant is that the species onion, as a whole, is ruled by, and vibrates to the keynote of, the fiery sign Aries. The impersonal soul's temporary need for expression has attracted it to this group of plants, and its original signature is largely obscured by the general vibratory rate of the species as a whole. The original signature is there were we but acute enough to perceive it; for undoubtedly plants of any species possess differences and individuality. But in our relation to them the group vibration is far more marked than their differences one from another; and in the case of plants ruled by Aries we expect them to be hot and irritating.

Applying the same thought to peoples, when we say that the English are ruled by Aries, we know that as a rule an Englishman will violently resent injury. But the individuals comprising the English nation have their own birth charts which indicate the celestial origin, the temperament, the abilities, and fortunes of each. Turning to animals, wolves likewise are ruled by Aries, and while some are quite different from others, yet all display the martial temperament. And still lower in the evolutionary scale we find among minerals, and possessing the characteristic qualities, brimstone also ruled by Aries.

Thus we find in each kingdom of life groups of entities that vibrate to the keynote of each of the zodiacal signs. To illustrate further let us consider the sign Taurus: In the mineral kingdom Taurus rules white coral, alabaster, all common white opaque stones, and the gem agate. In the vegetable kingdom it rules flax, larkspur, lilies, moss, spinach, myrtle, gourds, dandelion, daisies, columbine, colts-foot, plantain, and beets. In the animal kingdom Taurus rules those commonly known as bovine; the ox, cow, buffalo, yak, etc. Man, as a family, is ruled by Aquarius, but nations and towns have a distinct rulership. Thus the Irish people are ruled by Taurus, as are the cities of Dublin, Leipsic, St. Louis, Palermo, Parma, Mantua, and Rhodes. In like manner occupations, localities, physiological functions, anatomical parts, diseases, colors, tones, and various other classifications of things all have their signatures.

All nature, we find, is divided into seven distinct families, each family containing a membership on all planes and in each sphere of life. Further, the affinities of each family have a vibratory range that is not closely restricted, some members harmonizing more closely with the higher rates, and some members harmonizing more closely with the lower rates, of vibration within the range of the families affinities. Thus within the families groups are divided both by State of Life, and by Degree of Emanation. The planetary family of Mars, for instance, has affinities for two zodiacal signs. Aries belongs to the fiery state of life, first degree of emanation, while Scorpio belongs to the watery state of life, second degree of emanation.

Observation has shown that the influence of entities and groups upon each other very largely depends upon their vibratory rates, which in turn depend upon their signatures. Thus entities and groups belonging to the same planetary family have a vibratory quality similar to other members of the same family, although the plane occupied determines the octave from which the emanations proceed. In a similar manner there is a like vibratory quality between things ruled by the same zodiacal sign. Things ruled by the same planetary family, or by the same zodiacal sign, usually harmonize well. When the ruling signs are different but the celestial state is the same, as in the case of Taurus and Virgo, there is also pronounced harmony. Between things ruled by complementary states, that is, between fire and air, and between earth and water, there is a weak harmony. But between things ruled by contradictory states—between fire and water, and between air and earth—the vibrations are antagonistic and mutually destructive. These facts have an important bearing upon every phase of life.

Before indicating in detail just how everything we contact influences our lives for good or ill, and just how we have the power in great measure to control the influence of things over us by intelligently selecting our environment, let us for a moment consider that what is commonly called good and evil are but other names for harmony and discord.

Scarcely two people give these terms the same interpretation; for they are ever considered in relation to the ambitions and desires of the person using them, or are applied to other things the importance of which varies widely in the estimation of different people. Thus the thief, successful in his robbery, thinks this is good because it harmonizes with his desire for wealth. An honest man calls the act evil, because it is discordant to his idea of social responsibility. Again, a shower that is looked upon as good by agriculturists, may be called evil by the fashionable lady with whose house party it interferes. In the first instance it harmonized with the farmer's interest, in the second it was discordant to the house party. The rain was the same, but the thing influenced by it was different. Good and evil are terms that imply a relation to some definite entity. Insofar as an influence is harmonious to the entity it is called good, and insofar as it is discordant to the entity it is called evil. There is no good or evil aside from harmony and discord.

These entities which are influenced in a manner said to be good or evil are infinite in number and compose the universe. That is, the universe is composed of an infinite number of entities and groups of entities. They are all interacting and interdependent; everything, great and small, near and distant, has some influence, powerful or weak, upon every other thing in the universe. Whether the influence exerted by one thing upon another is good or evil depends upon the mutual harmony or mutual discord.

Better to understand the influence of things upon each other we should bear in mind not only that the law of gravitation is active between all objects in the universe, but that modern science demonstrates that all things radiate energy. Radium is the classical example of such radiation, but in a like manner, though much less pronounced, all substance is sending forth vibratory waves that can be detected at considerable distance by delicate scientific instruments. Aside from the controversy of the part the subject plays in diagnosing by the Electronic Reactions of Abrams, the Abrams method demonstrates conclusively that everything has a vibration to which it is keyed, and that these vibrations are radiated and can be detected at a distance. A number of experimenters have made marked improvements upon the original Abrams method, and have produced machines of great delicacy and accuracy in intercepting and interpreting the vibratory rates that all things radiate.

Were it not for energy radiated by objects and persons which in some manner leaves an impress upon all things coming close to them it seems unlikely that psychometry would be possible. Even sight depends, not upon the vibrations radiated by objects, but upon vibrations reflected from them. Such vibrations have an influence upon the human eye, different objects having a different influence. This difference in influence is due to diversity both in intensity and in form.

This leads to a very important consideration; for the intensity of influence tends to increase with the proximity of the object radiating it. It is true that things having the same vibratory rate that chance to vibrate synchronously—that is, the crest of the wave of one set of vibrations coinciding in time with the crest of the wave of the other set—are capable of influencing each other at great distances. A person changing his rate of vibration by raising or lowering it through altering his mood can illustrate this principle. In this manner he can get in rapport with people or things exceedingly remote, and having tuned in on their vibrations these may have greater influence upon him than other things with as great vibratory intensity close at hand. But aside from this factor of rapport the vibratory rates of things close at hand have a greater influence than the vibratory rates of similar things more distant. Likewise, even when rapport is established, a weaker vibration close at hand has as much influence as a stronger one radiated at a greater distance. To make practical application of this simply means the recognition that man is more influenced by the vibratory rates of things in his immediate environment than by those of somewhat similar nature more remote.

The manner in which man is thus influenced by the objects in his immediate environment is easily understood as soon as the general organization and makeup of his astral body, and its relation to the physical body are known.

The astral body, which is the mold of the physical body, is composed of astral substance organized by states of consciousness. The original planetary family, state of celestial life, and degree of emanation of a soul endow it with certain attractive and repulsive qualities. In the course of its involution to the mineral state, and its evolution from the mineral state to man these attractive and repulsive qualities attract it to incarnate in a great number of forms, in which it has a wide variety of experiences. Each experience affects the consciousness and is recorded as a mode of motion in the astral body. Thus the total experiences of a soul in its pilgrimage are recorded in the astral body. Through the law of affinity these energies within the astral body tend to unite where there is likeness and tend to segregate where there is unlikeness. Thus definite centers of energy are formed, each corresponding in its general vibratory rate to planetary influences, and other more general areas of the astral body are organized having vibrations corresponding to the zodiacal signs. Birth into human form, then, does not take place until the positions of the planets and signs—within certain limits—correspond to the vibratory organization of the astral body of the child to be born.

At birth the centers of energy already formed in the past through states of consciousness accompanying experiences are but intensified and given greater fixity. A person's character, as all must admit, is the sum total of all his past and present mental states. That is, they are the sum total of the states of consciousness organized as centers of energy within his astral form. These centers of energy are the mental factors both of the objective and the unconscious mind which determine the person's conduct. As the positions of the planets in the birth chart map these centers of energy, they constitute an accurate map of the character.

This map indicates with great accuracy, as shown by planetary positions, the general types of experience of the soul in its past. It indicates, by the prominence of the planets, the amount of the acquaintance the soul has had with experiences of each of the general types. It shows, by the aspects between the planets, the extent to which experiences of one type have been associated in the past with experiences of other types; and the extent to which these associations were harmonious or discordant. Furthermore, as the kind and amount of experiences attracted depend upon the original polarity of the soul when it started on its cyclic pilgrimage, if the map can rightly be interpreted, it should show the original signature of the soul, that is, the planetary family, the state of celestial life, and the degree of emanation, to which it belongs.

In its practical application, however, I believe great caution should be used in making positive assertions as to this, because the soul in incarnating has a fairly wide margin of vibratory rates within which incarnation is possible. That is, even as we must allow orbs of influence when considering aspects, so we must allow orbs of influence when considering the relation of the origin of the soul to the positions of the planets at birth. Thus a soul having its origin in the fiery state would tend when born in human form to have the sun in the birth chart in a fiery sign. But we may suppose in certain cases instead of the sun being in a fiery sign that there would be several other planets in fiery signs, and these planets strong in the birth chart. A soul belonging to a certain planetary family would certainly have this planet unusually prominent in the birth chart, and usually it would readily be picked as the most powerful planet in the chart, and consequently as the ruling planet. But we may suppose in a certain chart that while this planet is very powerful that there are other planets that seem quite as powerful, one of which might mistakenly be chosen as the true ruler of the chart. The experiences of a soul since its differentiation have been adding energies to its finer forms, and furthermore, the varied and unique requirements in the development of some souls to fit them for their work in the cosmic scheme of things is such as often to obscure the original equipment with which they started on their great cyclic journey.

We are quite justified in saying of a person in whose chart Jupiter is the dominant planet that he belongs to the planetary family of Jupiter. At the same time, due to the limitations that govern incarnation, if another planet, or more than one other planet, seems almost as strong, we cannot be positive that the soul did not have its origin in the family of this other planet. If the sun in a person's chart is in the sign Sagittarius we are quite justified in saying the individual belongs to the fiery state of life and the third degree of emanation. But if at the same time the moon, for instance, is rising in the sign Taurus, it might make it difficult to tell whether the soul had its origin in the fiery state, third degree, or in the earthy state and first degree of emanation ruled by Taurus.

This uncertainty which occasionally may arise need not seem discouraging; for in every known science, including physics, chemistry, and mathematics, we meet with problems no less disconcerting. Yet while the birth chart may not in our present state of knowledge tell us all about the parentage of the soul and its original environment in every instance, it does indicate infallibly the intensity, the kind, and the interrelations of the mental factors which comprise the character and determine the fortune.

It is these centers of energy within the astral form that give ability and that attract to the person the various events of his life. By the law of affinity like attracts like, and whatever vibrations and qualities reside, or are stimulated into activity, in the astral form attract corresponding conditions in the environment. A discordant vibratory center which in the past has been formed in association with procuring food and shelter will attract an environment that will make the procuring of these things, that is, the acquisition of wealth, most difficult. Such a center of energy would be indicated by Saturn afflicted in the Second House of the birth chart. Harmonious centers of energy as shown by the birth chart are actual forces within the astral body that attract an environment favorable to the department of life with which the center is shown to be associated. Thus fortune and misfortune, opportunity and lack of it, success and failure, are the results of centers of energy in the astral form which are infallibly shown in the birth chart. The birth chart gives the Astrological Signature in all its details.

It follows from these considerations that any modification of the centers of energy in the astral form make a corresponding change in the fortune. To the extent, then, that man can intelligently change the centers of energy within his astral form is he the master of his own destiny and free from blind fatality. These centers of energy with which he is born that are mapped by the birth chart are actually changed by three distinct factors.

As the planets move forward in the zodiac after a child's birth they make new aspects to their original positions in the birth chart and new aspects among themselves. These aspects thus formed store up energy that later is released by the cyclic motion of the heavens. These progressed positions of the planets, as they are called, stimulate and release energies in the astral form in directions and at times shown by the progressed aspects. Such releases of energy can be modified by the other factors to be considered, and their influence controlled by the selection of an environment suitable to their working out as indicated or in which they cannot work out as indicated. One factor, then, that changes the centers of energy in the astral body is the influence of the planets. This factor is fully discussed in Section 2 of Course 10, *Progressing the Horoscope*.

Another factor that changes the centers of energy within the astral body is the factor that originally organized them. That is, states of consciousness, or thought. How thought may be used to recondition the thought-cells of the astral body and thus bring about any desired change of fortune is explained in detail in Course 9, *Mental Alchemy*.

The third factor, and the one with which we here are more concerned, is the power of the objects in the environment to stimulate and modify by their radiations the centers of energy within the astral body and thus affect the life and destiny.

As previously explained each object and certain groups of objects, in fact, everything we contact from dense rock to human thought, is radiating energy. The type of energy radiated is determined by the astrological signature. In other words, everything vibrates in a key that corresponds to one of the celestial influences, and if this key is known its influence upon any other person or thing whose key is known can be predicted. The classical example of this power of vibration is the ability of a fiddler to fiddle a bridge down if he finds its key.

Now, within the astral body of man are centers of energy, some more prominent in some persons and some more prominent in other persons, that correspond to each of the various keys. When a person comes in contact with an object its vibrations stimulate a sympathetic response from the center of energy within the astral body that vibrates to its key. As everything we contact has a key of vibration, and radiates energy, each tends to stimulate centers of energy within the astral form. Every thing we contact gives additional activity to the center of energy mapped in the birth chart by the planet or sign ruling the object. If we know the astrological signature of things, then, we are aware of the particular center of energy in our astral forms that each stimulates into activity, and we may select such objects for our customary environment as will stimulate only those centers that we desire should become more active.

Some of these centers of energy are decidedly harmonious, and other centers are decidedly discordant, as shown by the aspects between the planets in the birth chart. Furthermore, some of them influence one department of life and others influence other departments of life, as shown by the house positions of the planets in the birth chart. To associate with the things that stimulate the discordant centers of energy gives these discordant centers additional power. The centers of energy within the astral form are modified in the direction of strengthening the discord, and the result is bound to be that added misfortune will enter the life. But to associate with the things that stimulate the harmonious centers of energy gives these harmonious centers additional power. Because the harmonious centers are so active they attract a more harmonious set of conditions into the life, which by their presence keep at a distance the events that the discordant centers otherwise would attract, and at the same time act positively to bring good fortune.

By selecting those centers of energy in the astral form that the birth chart shows are associated harmoniously with certain ambitions, and selecting the various objects and conditions of the environment that will add energy to these particular centers, it is possible to so change the power of these centers that they will act in a marked and positive manner to attract the object of the ambition. This is a practical application of the Law of Astrological Signatures the importance of which can hardly be over estimated.

Among the things that observation shows have a pronounced effect in changing the centers of energy within the astral form of persons closely associated with them are colors, tones, numbers, and names. Colors and tones have a vibration that in one case is visible and in the other case is audible. Names and numbers in themselves are abstract ideas, but when they enter the mind they give rise to

definite images which radiate energy through though
thought-waves vary with the name or number, and
associated with a person, or a house number or telephone n...
repeatedly thought about in connection with him by other persons,
keeps him bombarded with vibrations corresponding in rate to the
astrological signature of the name or number. These vibrations
change the centers of energy within his astral body in a definite way,
and bring about a change in his thoughts and in his fortune. The
influence of tones, colors, names, and numbers are treated in detail
in Course 6, *The Sacred Tarot.*

Localities also have their particular astrological signatures, their
specific vibrations which have the power to change the centers of
energy within the astral form and thus influence the life and destiny.
The rulership of the various kinds of localities is given in Chapter 5,
Course 8, *Horary Astrology.* Even the flowers with which we associate
have considerable influence, and gems which are worn have a great
influence over the life. The signatures of certain typical flowers, the
signatures of various gems, and the signature of letters, numbers,
colors, and tones are briefly given in Chapter 6, Course 10-1, *Delineating the Horoscope.*

A knowledge of astrological signatures is of utmost importance
in healing; for a treatment that one responds to, or a medicine that is
good for one person, may have an opposite effect when applied to
another person suffering with the same complaint. Methods of treatment each have their own signature, and are especially effective
when applied to patients of similar signature. Herbs and other
remedies likewise each have a specific vibration, and the effect of
their use depends upon the harmony or discord of corresponding
centers of energy in the astral body of the person to whom administered. A remedy ruled by a sign or planet stimulates the section
of the body corresponding to it in signature, and has a powerful
effect when applied to it. But if this section of the body is shown in
the birth chart to have a discordant vibration it but increases the
discord. A disease may successfully be treated by fighting and
overcoming its vibrations by the use of a remedy that is the vibratory
antidote. This is on the principle that water quenches fire. Or it may
be treated by applying to the afflicted part a remedy ruled by the
celestial influence in the birth chart that makes the strongest harmonious aspect to the part afflicted. By thus strengthening the part
where the affliction occurs with additional harmony the disease,
which is an inharmonious condition, can no longer manifest. These,

however, are considerations that are discussed in Course 16, *Stellar Healing*.

Perhaps there is no department of life in which the doctrine of signatures plays a more important part than in our association with others. The centers of energy within the astral body of each person are radiating energy. Some of these centers radiate harmonious energy and some of them radiate discordant energy. Thus when we come in close contact with another person our astral bodies receive the impact of these vibrations, and our centers of energy are greatly stimulated. But the manner in which they are stimulated depends, in great measure, not merely upon the harmony of these centers considered separately, but upon the natural harmony or discord that obtains between the centers of energy in one person's astral body as related to the centers of energy in the astral body of the other person. A comparison of birth charts indicates quickly just how one person will affect another if they become closely associated, and in just what department of life, and how, the harmony or discord will manifest.

For harmony in marriage the first consideration is that the etheric vibrations, as shown chiefly by the First House and the Moon should be similar. If markedly dissimilar their energies will not fuse, they will not get in complete rapport, and both will experience a constant feeling of unrest and dissatisfaction. The next consideration should be that both belong to the same planetary family, or at least that the mental trend should be enough alike that they have interests in common. Finally, if both belong to the same state of life, or to complementary states, as shown by the sun signs, it enables them to understand each other's viewpoint, leading to compatibility. This subject is treated in detail in Chapters 6 and 7, Course 10-1, *Delineating the Horoscope*.

Another department of life over which the doctrine of signatures has a profound influence is business and the acquisition of wealth. Each person has within his astral body a center of energy, as shown by his birth chart, that vibrates more strongly to some natural source of wealth than do the other centers. In other words, things of a certain type attract to him wealth that he could not hope to attract in association with other things. Therefore, to the extent he associates with things that correspond in nature to his most harmonious center of energy will he attract wealth, and to the extent he associates with the things that correspond to the most discordant center of energy in his astral body will he meet financial misfortune.

The astrological signature of a person indicates the type of ability he has. He should capitalize on this ability by following a business, trade, or profession where it is called into play. But if he would succeed to his utmost, in the use of this ability he should find an avenue of its expression in which he is constantly brought in contact with the things corresponding to the most harmonious center in his astral body; for they are his natural sources of wealth.

The doctrine of signatures in its practical application has a ramification as wide as the interests of man. It pervades, and has an important bearing in, the most unexpected quarters. The student of the occult will meet it at every step. Only through a knowledge of this doctrine, as here most briefly outlined, can man live to his highest, accomplish most for himself and for others, and become of utmost service to universal society.

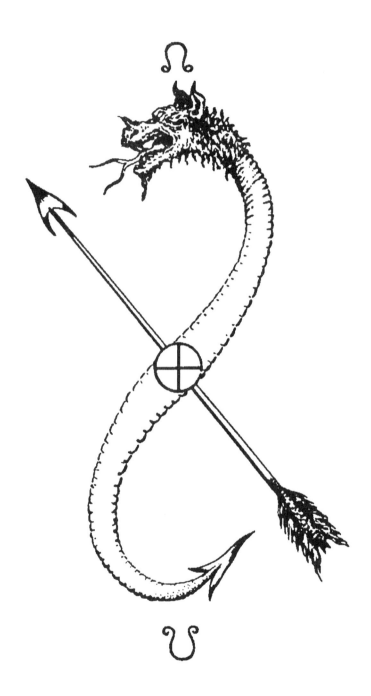

Chapter 7

Facts and Fancies
About Reincarnation, Part 1

O VER the Occident has swept from dreamy Oriental skies, during the past forty-five years, a balmy breeze of metaphysical speculation laden with the aroma of the choicest flowers of eastern thought. Upon the West it has had a salutary influence, warming the chill winds that blow so constantly from the icebergs of the practical that they threaten to force upon us a frigid climate of materialism.

The more spiritual inhabitants of the Occident were quick to recognize the advantages to be derived from the East, and opened wide the windows of their souls to the genial influx, absorbing often without discrimination all that the aromatic zephyrs wafted to their shores. Unfortunately, the flowers of Oriental thought are not all friendly to the human race; for amid the wholesome varieties whose perfumes become an invigorating tonic to the spiritual nature are to be found others noxious, whose noisome odors poison and atrophy the soul. Another efflorescence, the subject of this lesson, scarce less deadly in character, has a most fascinating fragrance that intoxicates as a subtle stimulus. Its effect is to interest in things spiritual, to give high ideals and lofty aspirations; but at the same time to dim the spiritual sight and confuse the mind. It numbs the senses of the soul by refuting their evidence, and sinks the intellect into a state of dull apathy where, rather than make the effort to acquire knowledge at first hand, it is content blindly to accept the statements of others.

So thoroughly has western occultism become intoxicated with this insidious teaching of human reincarnation and karma that one scarcely can open a book upon occult subjects without finding some reference to it within a few pages, its verity being taken as a matter of course. Occult periodicals teem with references to it, and one seldom mentions a phenomenon in which occult forces play a part without being called upon to explain its relation to reincarnation. Upon the shelves of our public libraries are volumes written to prove its truth, but strangely enough, we find little there analyzing it or criticizing it. The student upon his first approach to occult science is impressed generally with the notion that he must accept unquestioningly the dogma of human reincarnation as the foundation of truth if he is to accept any part of occult teachings. So fully has this subtle doctrine permeated western esoterics that few have the hardihood to express their opinions if these are contrary to the popular current. It is so firmly entrenched that anyone daring to present the opposite side of the question is, if possible, immediately squelched, discredited, and made an object of discountenance and suspicion.

Now, I am convinced it is a most dangerous omen when people permit themselves to be so dominated by any new idea, religious or political, that they fear to hear it criticized. It is an augur of approaching mental slavery. Prohibiting critical investigation has been the method employed through countless ages by religious and political autocracies, and where successful has never failed effectually to block the path of mental and spiritual progress. Error must ever be hedged and protected by a wall of prejudice and intolerance, but truth is strong enough to withstand in the open the assault of mental conflict.

Before saying more, that my position may not be misinterpreted, I may mention that among those I esteem highly are students who make human reincarnation the groundwork of their belief. Others equally esteemed are steeped in the tenets of the various orthodox sects. Nevertheless, these people are intellectual, and they are clever in applying occult forces and in discerning occult truths that do not happen to conflict with their religious preconceptions. These good friends are morally worthy, possess high ideals, and are prompted by the best of motives.

Then again, there undoubtedly have been Christian Mystics who have believed devoutly in vicarious atonement, and there have been Oriental Mystics accepting reincarnation, who have been of unparalleled virtue and goodness. So today there are many worthy persons in both classes. And it is not my desire in issuing this lesson to wound the sensibilities of these who hold to ideas at variance with my own, or to imply, upon their part, lack of intelligence. I do, however, feel in duty bound to exercise the prerogative necessary to mental freedom; the right of honest disagreement between scientific investigators.

It has been well said that it is easier to rescue truth from error than from confusion. Science and philosophy have found it no difficult task to overthrow falsity once there is something tangible to grasp. But a hazy chimera presents no secure hold for the reason. Could the tenets of human reincarnation be sharply defined it could be grappled straightway and its strength proved. But there is nothing definite about it; for in scarcely two schools are the same things taught, and those advocating it most persistently do not agree in its essential details.

The number of incarnations in human form necessary are given by Mr. Sinnett, who was the first to publish anything regarding the appointed number of reincarnations, as not less than 686, and normally not far short of 800, but varying within narrow limits. One strong school in America teaches that two or three incarnations are all that are necessary, and various other centers teaching reincarnation range between these figures.

As to the time elapsing between incarnations we find in Mr. Sinnett's Esoteric Buddhism that rebirth in less than 1500 years is spoken of as almost impossible. But a prominent school in France, whose teachings are gaining ground in America, teaches it not to be uncommon for one to reincarnate in the offspring of his own child and thus be his own grandparent. The teachings fluctuate between these extremes, the most generally accepted in America at present being perhaps that about 500 years elapses between rebirths.

The precise effect of karma also is the subject of much discussion, some leaders of the old school holding that the evil wrought in one life returns only in a general way in a future life, while many of the newer teachers insist on a specific reaction of the good or evil—that a murderer will be murdered in a future life by his former victim, etc.

In addition to this indefiniteness, which makes plausible explanations easy because almost anything may happen in so wide a range of possibilities, there are woven about these doctrines, by the morbid imaginations of semi-lucid mystics who pose as teachers and thus find their way into print, such fantastic fabrics of illusion as were never dreamed of by that most erudite founder of Theosophy, H.P. Blavatsky, who was instrumental in introducing reincarnation to the West. Lacking definite information concerning the theories they are taught, the minds of many students become filled with hazy and ill-defined notions. Such phantasy thinking conduces to a negativeness in which they become unwittingly easily influenced by unseen malign forces.

Because it has received so much publicity, the investigator, at the beginning of his studies is usually impressed with the idea that reincarnation is accepted unquestionably by all occultists at the present day who have progressed far along the path, and that it has been the universal belief of all notable reformers, philosophers, and initiates of the past.

As a single example, from innumerable instances that might be cited, of the method by which the beginner in occult studies is impressed that everyone, not only of the present day, but also in the past, who has been noted for wisdom has embraced the doctrine of human reincarnation, it is commonly and stoutly asserted that the doctrine is taught in the Bible, and by the Master, Jesus.

Now it is a current saying, based on the controversies of some two hundred Christian Sects, that anything can be proved upon Biblical authority. But to believe that a considerable part of the earth's inhabitants have studied the Bible for nineteen hundred years without discerning that human reincarnation is one of its fundamental and important teachings, if that teaching is really there, oversteps the bounds of average credulity.

It is cited commonly, in support of the contention that reincarnation is taught in the Bible, that Jesus answered Nicodemus—John 3:3—saying:

> 3. Verily, verily, I say unto thee, Except a man be born again, he cannot see the kingdom of God.

Those who quote this in favor of the doctrine of human reincarnation fail, however, to mention the verses that follow this answer:

> 4. Nicodemus saith unto Him, How can a man be born when he is old? Can he enter the second time into his mother's womb, and be born?
> 5. Jesus answered, Verily, verily, I say unto thee, Except a man be born of water and of the Spirit, he cannot enter into the kingdom of God.
> 6. That which is born of the flesh is flesh; and that which is born of the spirit is spirit.
> 7. Marvel not that I say unto thee, Ye must be born again.
> 8. The wind bloweth where it listeth, and thou hearest the sound thereof, but canst not tell whence it cometh, and whither it goeth:

so is every one that is born of the Spirit.

Jesus tells Nicodemus, as plainly as possible, that he must have a spiritual birth. Certainly He could not be explaining the doctrine of human reincarnation in such language. And if He even believed in it He certainly failed in his mission as a teacher. He made his doctrines of Love your Neighbor, and Do unto others as You would have them Do unto You, so plain that they were understood by the most ignorant and by the most innocent, as well as by the learned. But if He had ideas on human reincarnation He expressed them so poorly that the greatest scholars in the world during nineteen hundred years failed to discover them.

Another attempt to warp a plain Biblical statement into such form that it appears to uphold a pernicious doctrine is the citation in regard to the transfiguration in Math. 17:12,13:

But I say unto you, that Elias is come already, and they knew him not, but have done unto him whatsoever they listed. Likewise also shall the Son of Man suffer of them.
Then the disciples understood that he spake unto them of John the Baptist.

The obvious thought here conveyed is that John the Baptist carried out the ideas of Elias; for Elias and Moses appeared at the transfiguration talking to Jesus. Yet if Elias had incarnated as John the Baptist, he would now be John the Baptist, and no longer be Elias or appear as Elias. John the Baptist had already been beheaded; and if Elias and John the Baptist were one, John the Baptist being the last incarnation would have appeared at the transfiguration, not as Elias, but as John. As Elias, according to the narrative, was the one to appear, that is proof positive that Elias retained his individuality as Elias and had not reincarnated as John.

As a matter of fact, the personal investigations of an increasing number of Western Initiates, including the author and many others who have undergone special training necessary for such research, all go to disprove the theory of human reincarnation. At no time in its history has The Brotherhood of Light held to this doctrine. Further, among the independent thinkers scattered over the West—those astrologers, psychics, and occultists who do not bow to statements based merely upon authority—there is a rapidly diminishing number adhering to it. Even in India, the home of its birth, it is far from a universal belief, and is stoutly denied by many learned Hindu Initiates.

It should be borne in mind that there is a vast difference between the doctrine of reincarnation and that of human reincarnation. Reincarnation as applied to the soul in its evolution through various progressive forms from mineral up to man, has been almost a universal tenet in the occult schools, and reference to it may be found in the sacred and philosophical writings of all ages. From this fact confusion has arisen; for the human reincarnation school has construed every reference to reincarnation made by any writer of consequence to mean human reincarnation, which is an entirely different doctrine, and strenuously denied by Western Initiates.

Human reincarnation implies that once incarnated as man and gaining self-consciousness in the human state, the soul must repeatedly return and animate other human bodies. Most ancient schools of occultism, including The Brotherhood of Light, believe in reincarnation through various progressive species, but they deny the doctrine of human reincarnation.

That it is not taught by Western Initiates is evidenced by the writings of H. P. Blavatsky who introduced human reincarnation to America. According to her own testimony, "I first worked under the Egyptian part of the African section and later under the Indian section."

While writing *Isis Unveiled* she worked largely under the direction of Western Initiates, and in various places in the original edition of that work stoutly denies human reincarnation. *Isis Unveiled*, Vol. I, p. 351, reads:

> Reincarnation, i.e., the appearance of the same individual, or rather his astral monad, twice on the same planet, is not a rule in nature; it is an exception, like the teratological phenomena of a two-headed infant.

Again, she says that when it does occur the designs of nature have been interfered with and she must make another effort, but—

> If reason has been so far developed as to become active and discriminative, there is no reincarnation on this earth, for the three parts of the triune man have been united together, and he is capable of running the race.

Those are precisely the views held by Western Initiates and it was not until removing her headquarters to India and coming directly in contact with Hindu teachers that H.P.B. finally accepted the doctrine of human reincarnation. Ample testimony of this is to be found in *Old Diary Leaves*, by H. C. Olcott, President-founder of the Theosophical Society, who was the constant companion and co-worker of H.P.B. during the time she was writing *Isis Unveiled*. Mr. Olcott says:

> I believe she wrote then as she did later, exactly according to her lights, and that she was just as sincere in denying reincarnation in 1876—1878 as she was in affirming it after 1882. H.P.B. revisited Simla without me in 1881, and the two friends above mentioned (Mr. Sinnett and Mr. A. C. Hume) received in due time from the Masters the Reincarnation theory. Mr. Sinnett expounded it in Fragments No. 4 (Theosophist, Vol. IV, No. 1, October, 1882), where he laid the basis of the doctrine of Terrestrial Reincarnation.

This was seven years after the founding of the Theosophical Society and six years after the date of Mr. Olcott's conversation in New York with a Mahatma, in which reincarnation was convincingly denied. I do not doubt, therefore, that H.P.B. was sincere; for while working under the Western Initiates she denied reincarnation, but after her removal to India her mediumistic nature, which was remarkably pronounced, absorbed and became enamored with the doctrine by which she then was environed. The dogmas of her later associates, whose minds had been trained for magic, invaded her mentality despite her previous training.

Returning to the occult student's first impressions; he is informed that a large portion of the globe's inhabitants believe in human reincarnation. This is sadly true, even as in Galileo's day most of the people, including the learned, believed the world flat. In fact, the multitude in times past have mostly been outrageously wrong. And there is no assurance that at the present day they constitute a competent jury to pass a verdict upon truth.

Neither is it wise to place reliance upon the claims to knowledge of others; for history is a chronicle of mistaken authority. The only safe plan is to keep the mind open until such time as one can evolve the necessary faculties to prove truth at first hand, keeping in mind that the mediumistic tendencies of the human race are such that whatever political, religious, or moral ideas are held by a few dominant minds are usually accepted by the rest without criticism or analysis. Thus nations are subject to waves for war, for peace, for reform, and for various other things, and few stop to consider how they are carried along on the mental tide without adequate reason. They are possessed of a new set of ideas, often made plausible by the flimsiest arguments, that instantly blot out their former convictions.

Such an argument in favor of reincarnation is the appeal to the principle of justice, a principle firmly seated within the human breast. Man is reluctant to believe the Creator unjust, and ardently seeks some method of reconciling the apparent injustices perpetrated by nature. At first glance human reincarnation seems to solve the problem of these inequalities of life. But a closer scrutiny reveals that it has completely failed to give a reasonable solution as does a belief in the whims and caprices of the Jewish Jehovah.

In the first place, if we use these inequalities as material for argument, their value must be ascertained. If they possess real value the inequalities are real, but if their value is indeterminate, so also must be the inequalities.

Now the materialist stoutly affirms that health, wealth, honor, intellect, etc., which form the apparent inequalities of life, are of real value. The occultist, on the other hand, maintains that the real man is spiritual and immortal, that external experiences have no value in themselves, but are the means through which real values for the soul may be created. That is, an experience may be made the means of spiritual progress, but this value lies not in the experience, but in the soul's attitude toward it. Consequently, as even the worst calamities may be made a means of soul progression, these also may be made valuable.

Thus it is a matter of common observation that hardships, trials, and sorrows are more readily turned into values of progress than the so-called good fortunes. Few ever turn their faces toward the rising sun of spirituality until they have drained the cup of adversity to the dregs. The successful man, all too often, is too absorbed by business cares, the wealthy woman by social ambitions or pleasures, the man of science in his work, to care for higher things. And so, not infrequently, those materially fortunate are spiritually cursed.

If we admit that events in themselves possess value we should incline to the view that the severest and most painful experiences have the greatest value, and that the Scriptures are correct in implying that whomsoever the Lord loveth He chastiseth. From this viewpoint we are compelled to draw the conclusion that material advantages are the worst punishment inflicted by divine justice; for scarcely shall a rich man enter into the kingdom of heaven. This completely reverses the popular conception of karma, and would indicate that the prosperous man is now paying by his prosperity for some heinous crime committed in a past life.

But with Socrates, Epicretus, Aurelius, and a host of other thinkers, I am unwilling to admit the value of events in themselves. I hold that good may be derived from any event of life by utilizing it for progress, in which case the value lies not in the event, but in the soul's attitude. So, what is used by one soul for progress is by another permitted to become a hindrance, no two probably needing the same experiences to develop their latent possibilities, nor would they make the same progress under the same circumstances. Let us not forget that the spiritual geniuses of the past have had their soul powers forged in the furnace of material affliction. To them adversity proved a great blessing. From this it might be thought that for good deeds one should be rewarded in the next life by the direst of circumstances and be made the subject of severest persecutions. But all souls might not respond alike to such vigorous treatment. No doubt there are some weak ones who need the tender hot-house care of material blessings, though these seem at a disadvantage and seldom make a thrifty spiritual growth.

Viewed from the physical plane, we now see that the good consists of material and objective advantages, but that viewed from the plane of spirit the good consists of such subjective and spiritual advantages as are usually found in deadly conflict with advantages material. These two ideas of good antagonize. One cannot at the same time worship God and Mammon. They are just as opposite as the sun viewed from the earth, and the earth viewed from the sun. As a consequence of this dual viewpoint, the spiritual philosopher might accuse the Creator of injustice if he were born in easy circumstances, while the materialist might bewail his fate if born in humble surroundings. From this it must be plain that the popular conception of Karmic Law—reward and punishment meted out in terms of material advantages—is purely and completely a materialistic doctrine.

Returning now to a logical standpoint: All must admit that viewing it from the angle of soul progression we are unable to say, in any particular case, which are the good events and which the evil; for an event that is utilized by one soul may prove a hindrance to another. An event at one period of life may produce an opposite effect than if experienced at a different time. It will be seen, then, that any just system of reward must be based upon the momentary needs of the soul. And who shall say, at any given time, what experiences will advance the soul furthest in the long run and help it evolve its latent attributes? The experiences of life meet the transitory and constantly shifting requirements of the soul, but the apparent inequalities of this life—which of itself is but the tick of the second hand on the watch timing the soul's infinite flight—these inequalities, I affirm, are indeterminate.

Another purely materialistic conception is the idea that nowhere in the vastness of the boundless universe can justice be meted out except on this speck of dust called earth. Millions of worlds crowd space, larger and grander than ours; electromagnetic, astral, and spiritual worlds, as well as those material. Planes interpenetrate planes, all swarming with intelligent life. The world of matter is concrete to our physical senses, but not so in reality. The electrons of matter are comparable—relative to their size in proportion to their distances—to the planets of our solar system. Electromagnetic, astral, and spiritual worlds are as real and tangible to the senses of their denizens as is the earth to man. In fact, as is the testimony of the many exalted souls who temporarily freed from the body have visited that glorious realm, the spiritual world is a world of increased consciousness.

So, too, the astral spheres surrounding the earth are fully as actual as the material world. There the sensations of pleasure and pain are far more intense than those in the physical. Then why should the physical world be the only place where man can expiate his errors? The experiences of seers, prophets, and initiates testify that in the spheres interior to the physical man has every opportunity for atonement and purification, and every facility for progress. That the doctrine of Karma as taught finds a following at all seems to me to be due to the difficulty many have, even as they cannot imagine a country with different customs, of conceiving any reality beyond their immediate experience.

Then again, a system of morals based upon doing good for reward, either in this life or the next, is at heart a system of selfishness. And to hold that the earth is the only place where divine justice can be administered is materialistic. Yes! It is worse than materialistic; for materialism at least offers the encouragement of oblivion after death. But human reincarnation blights all hope by dooming to innumerable lives—with all their agonies and heartaches, amid worldly conditions that already have become to the pure in heart a hell of avarice, selfishness, sensuality, and carnal desire—in human form.

What, then, may we consider the cause of the apparent inequalities of life? They are the result of the quality and nature of each soul harmonizing with or antagonizing its environment.

It attracts to itself an environment corresponding in vibratory rate to the thought-cells present in the astral body with which it has clothed itself. These thought-cells have been organized by its various experiences in lower forms of life. Experiences of a certain type impress their influence upon the sensitive astral form as a definite organization of energy. This organization of energy persists in the astral form when it is attracted to and becomes incarnated in a higher species of life and tends to attract it to experiences of a similar type. If the experiences have been inharmonious, it tends by vibratory affinity to attract other discordant experiences; but if the experiences were harmonious, it tends to attract other harmonious experiences of the same type.

The soul, in its involution through higher worlds, and its evolution through life-forms from mineral to man, attracted to itself experiences of a given kind because of its original polarity—its original quality of vibration. This original attractive and repellent quality arose at the differentiation of the soul as the result of cosmic need. That is, there was the need for a soul of definite qualities in the universal scheme of things, and this universal need, this void to be filled, through the agency of its angelic parents, gave the soul its basic trend.

The influence of the thought-cells organized by experience is beautifully illustrated in astrology. The planets are not the cause of a person's condition in life. They merely correspond to the thought-cells in his astral form. These thought-cells, and their organization within his finer bodies, are his character. His character, therefore, because of the strong and weak, harmonious and discordant desires of its thought-cells, attracts to him the conditions and events of his life.

To be sure, these conditions and events are shown in the astrological birth chart, but only because a child is not born until its vibrations correspond with the vibratory rates received upon the earth from the planets. After birth the planets send him energies that have an influence upon his actions, just as the weather and other factors of his physical environment also have an influence upon his actions. But it is really the activities of thought-cells within his astral form that attract conditions and events, the positions of the planets, by their stations and aspects, mapping these activities in the astral body. If they are harmonious, they denote prosperity, but if discordant, they signify adversity.

The fortune of a person, then, is the affect of the environment thus attracted reacting upon the character. And a character that is a martyr in one age, in another might be an object of adoration. A tyrant born at an opportune time and place might rise to the throne, while in a different environment might as quickly mount the scaffold.

Human reincarnation would have us believe the martyr suffered torture because of sins in some past life, and the successful tyrant was given the power to scourge him to the flames because of good done in some remote incarnation. But the very good fortune of the tyrant in this life leads to actions, as material fortune often does, that will make him an object of commiseration in the future. I am loath to think the spiritual giants who have left their footprints on the sands of time have endured the suffering which has been their common heritage in expiation of past misdeeds; or that wealthy parasites, living in luxury upon the very heart's blood of the poor, are thus being rewarded for beneficence in ages gone.

Instead, I must adopt the old Hermetic teaching that, even as children on earth have physical parents, so do souls at their differentiation, before their descent into matter, have angelic parents. These angelic parents are not the creators of souls; but by their parenthood offer the conditions for souls to enter the grand cycle of necessity.

Souls, then, are differentiated by angelic parents in response to a definite universal need, and each is sent out to be educated to perform a required function in universal affairs. Its inherent character, persisting potentially from the moment of its differentiated existence as an entity, and determined by the universal need that called it into differentiated existence, endows it with definite attractive and repulsive qualities. Because of this basic polarity which it acquired at the moment of differentiation, during its cyclic journey down through spiritual and astral realms, and then evolving up through various forms from mineral to man, it is attracted more strongly to certain phases of life than to others. It is the qualities thus developed in lower impersonal forms, persisting as thought-cells within the astral body, that tend to attract events and environment of corresponding quality, harmony or discord, when the soul finally incarnates as man.

Now, a little observation will show that the object of Nature in life is diversity of expression, not identical expression. The requirements of universal life need souls of various qualities, even as civilization requires men and women adapted to many trades and professions. All men are not fitted to be artists, or musicians; and it is well that they are not, for the world needs those skilled in mechanics and those who produce food. Neither have souls the same destiny. All are essential in the cosmic scheme, and find their greatest joy in doing their appointed tasks. Blessed are they when they have found their work! And who shall say what is great and what is small in this universal scheme of things, or whom are the important ones? Should the hand criticize the foot for lack of equal dexterity, or the eye be envious of the ear, or the heart feel it has been unjustly treated because it is not given the work of the lungs?

Souls differ as do the trees in the forest, not alone in magnitude, but as to their ultimate goal. Mature trees represent the kind of seed planted plus the environment since planting. A human represents the inherent nature of the soul plus its experiences while involving and while ascending through various forms from mineral up to man. But no environment will make a fir tree grow from an acorn, nor a soul springing from the planetary family of Saturn into an aggressive warrior. Oaks, firs, cedars, and fruit trees, each have an economic value. It would be difficult to say which is of most importance. Each species also differs in the size and quality of individuals. So also souls springing from the same family, state of spiritual life, and degree of emanation, differ one from another. Not only may they have different angelic parents, but their experiences previous to human incarnation may widely differ. Consequently, when they arrive at the human stage of their pilgrimage their educational needs, in order to round out their latent qualifications for universal usefulness, are very different.

The character at birth is the result of the soul's past experiences reacting on its inherent quality, just as the character of a horse or a dog is likewise the result of past incarnations in still lower forms. That a man must have had innumerable human incarnations because he has a brilliant intellect is tantamount to saying a race horse must have had innumerable incarnations as a horse—at times being a wild horse, a farm horse, a dray horse, a buggy horse,—etc. in order to be a race horse. Or must we say that a setter must have passed incarnations as a mongrel, a terrier, a hound, a coach dog, etc.? Not so! The soul never incarnates in the same species twice. It is ever drawn to a species higher in the scale of evolution. It is a dog but once, and whether a cur or a life-saving New Foundland depends upon its transitory need for experience. A horse will be a horse but once, but whether a plug or a driver will depend upon its incidental polarity, and has nothing whatever to do with its sins or good deeds to other horses in past lives.

Likewise, the soul inhabits the physical form of man but once; and whether as a Bushman or a college professor depends upon its transitory need for expression. Then it passes to a higher form in the scale of evolution, which in this case is a spiritual form. To say that each man needs all possible experiences and all kinds of human lives is to assume that Nature's aim is identity of expression. But Nature's aim, as a glance around must assure us, is specialization. This principle of division of labor and specialization of parts, as well as the development of individualism, is glaringly apparent in all her work.

Nor is the disparity between races of mankind so great as was formerly thought. The science of language has in later years made this plain. Even the Australian Bushman, when given the same educational advantages, is found to rival his European brother in attainment; although, of course, following the law of specialization, each race more readily becomes proficient in certain lines. But among human beings there are not, as among animals and birds and plants, different families, different genera, and different species. All belong to a single species—Homo Sapiens—the various sub-species, or races, being due, as sub-species usually are, to the affect of local environment.

Certainly, the savagery practiced in modern warfare by civilized nations cannot be surpassed by the aborigines of any land. The love of pillage is just as strong in the breasts of our millionaires as in those of the lowly savage. To be sure, the average savage follows a stricter code of morals than that to be found in our populous centers of civilization. And it should be remembered that intellect is no mark of spirituality; for the intellectual geniuses have all too often been the scourges of mankind.

At first glance it would seem that the savage labored under a great disadvantage; but when we consider that responsibility can only be measured by opportunity, and that the savage usually makes as much of his opportunities as the civilized man, if not more, it alters our conception. For karma, if just, must deal lightly with those who err through ignorance, while punishing severely those who know the right and deliberately forsake it for the wrong. Yet where knowledge of spiritual things is concerned, the savage usually has the best of it; for living close to Nature he draws from her the knowledge of a spiritual life and frequently communes with the dead, while civilized man, having his inner senses blunted by artificial living, scoffs at all his dollars cannot buy.

The savage, therefore, when he passes to the life after physical death will have but a few foolish notions and fetishes to forget. But the civilized man will be encumbered by a thousand false scientific and religious teachings, as well as the fetish of his egotism. He usually is so sure nothing can lie beyond his preconceptions that he will free himself from them only with great difficulty.

But what narrow vision is it that would single out from the illimitable chain of existences that forms the cycle of the soul, this particular link of destiny as the only one needing consideration in the light of divine justice? Is the horse that is whipped, or the dog that is starved and beaten, or the deer wounded in the chase, so tortured because of sins committed in the past? If we look about us we find that suffering is Nature's means of furthering evolution; for suffering is the common heritage of life as we observe it. The rose grows thorns and the cactus develops spines to escape the pain inflicted by foraging beasts. Man builds a new machine to escape the suffering of arduous toil. We all have suffered in the lower kingdoms. To single out what a man suffers here, or what he gains here, from what he has gained in the past, and what lies before him in the superb vistas of the future, is to try to judge the size and splendor of a mountain range by looking at a single pebble.

Those who die young grow to maturity and are given all the opportunities for progress in the astral world. The mission of external life is to develop self-consciousness, and that once attained there is ample opportunity in higher spheres for further development. Whatever is necessary for the development and culture of man can be found there. A savage or a child can be taught there quite as readily as here.

It may be asked, then, of what use is external life if its lessons can be learned elsewhere. It is a necessary experience for the realization of self-consciousness. But even as an animal species is one link in the evolutionary chain, and the soul incarnating in it passes at death to the next higher form regardless of whether it lived in Africa or

America, whether it lived a few days, or for years, or whether it was permitted all the experiences common to the species or not; so man at death passes on in his evolution, even though on earth much restricted. And he will find, to recompense him for loss of opportunity on earth, other advantages on the next plane.

If a man's miseries are due to karma resulting from sin, in his first incarnation when he had no evil karma he must have had all opportunities, all happiness, all blessings. It is surprising under such conditions that he should ever have sinned and brought the vengeance of suffering upon his head. Apparently everyone is sinking deeper in the mire of sin, for suffering is everywhere prevalent. And if we could not escape sin when we were free from malignant karma, how can we expect to live blameless lives with the weight of it now like millstones about our necks?

If we explain human suffering and lack of opportunity by referring it to the just action of karma, we are then called upon to explain the justice of the equally great suffering and inequalities of the animal world. When man is born into human form the first time he has had no moral karma, for like the animals he has been previously irresponsible. But animals suffer in spite of their lack of karma, and animals of the same species have unequal opportunities. It is only when man attains self-consciousness and becomes morally responsible that he can make good or evil karma. Therefore, as in his first appearance on earth he had previously been an irresponsible agent, he could have had no evil karma. His condition then must have been determined by something besides karma. What this is that determined man's condition in his first incarnation reincarnationists do not tell us. But certainly it is preposterous to suppose that all men in their first incarnation are born with the same or equal characters and opportunities, in equal environments, and undergo equal suffering. Nowhere in Nature do we observe any such equal condition. Is it not more probable then, that the same factors that determine an animal's condition of life also determined man's?

Even could it be shown that all people in their first incarnation had equal opportunities and equal happiness, there would yet remain to be explained the great injustice that gives to one person a character at his first human incarnation—before the intervention of karma—that enables him to triumph over evil and avoid generating much evil karma; while giving to another a weak and feeble character that has not the power to resist evil, and thus accumulates a terrific karmic burden. Before the intervention of this karma the individual could not have been responsible for the kind of character he possessed. But if characters were equal and opportunities were equal, experiences would be equal, and we would not witness the apparent inequalities that we daily observe. So, after all, that a soul is endowed with a weak character before attaining responsibility would seem as great an injustice as that of being given poor opportunities.

The justice of difference in character which, to account for the differences to be observed in lives, must be admitted if it be held that advantages are meted out justly, can only be explained by the obvious fact that there is need for various kinds of souls who undergo different experiences. Karma plays no part as a moral agent until moral responsibility is attained. Man is ushered into life once without such karma, then, and subject to the very inequalities karma was invented to explain. Numerous lives only increase the suffering, for suffering is common to physical life, none being entirely free from it. Karma serves no real purpose and removes the hope of being free from this suffering to a remote future. To justify the suffering of one life, reincarnationists have substituted equally unjust suffering through many hundred lives. Unjust, because in nearly all cases the one punished is entirely ignorant of why he is suffering. It is as if a man were to whip a grown dog for offenses committed when he was a puppy.

Karma has no power to force man back upon earth. Nature does not reverse her operations. The soul on the ascending arc of evolution cannot reincarnate in a lower form, nor can it thwart the purpose of the life-wave by repeatedly reincarnating in any one species of life. The life-wave carries man irresistibly to the next stage, which is above the physical. Karma really embraces the astral organizations which we have built into our astral bodies previous to and during earthly life. These, by the law of magnetic affinity, after death attract us to conditions corresponding to their vibratory rates and compel us to work out our redemption from evil face to face with the motive prompting every earthly deed, with conscience presiding as the judge.

The factors that determine man's condition in life when born into human form, are the original polarity of the soul, plus the various thought-cells organized in the astral form through his experiences in the lower forms of life through which he has evolved. His condition at any time during human life is determined by the organizations of energy in his astral form at birth, plus those added by the various thoughts and deeds up to the time considered. Likewise, his condition immediately after death is determined by the thought-cells organized in his astral body up to the time of death. As morality or lack of it is most effective during human life in power to give these thought-cells special desires, atonement is not a matter of vengeance. It is a purification preparatory to a higher phase of life in which, if there is suffering, there is full knowledge of what caused it. We find, therefore, that human reincarnation as usually taught is illogical, unjust, purely speculative, hope destroying, and completely materialistic.

It is an orthodox teaching of the Orient; and orthodox beliefs of both East and West were formulated in a period when men knew almost nothing about how Nature operates. How Nature is actually observed to perform, the Universal Law of Compensation, and the true significance of pleasure and pain are explained in Course 19, *Organic Alchemy.*

Facts and Fancies
About Reincarnation, Part 2

_____

A LL the evidence put forward as proof of human reincarnation, insofar as it has come to my attention, is, I feel confident, but a misinterpretation of actual facts. I have no occasion to question the honesty of the witnesses. They without doubt report what is seen and what is felt as it seems to them. But as these experiences are invariably of a psychic nature, they must be interpreted in the light of what is known to be the conditions imposed upon psychically received information. When so interpreted they prove, not human reincarnation, but certain laws governing psychic phenomena.

As an example from many: An elderly lady and her companion were traveling through the state of Minnesota when the engine broke down and the train could not move for several hours. Although she had never been in the state before, she felt an intimate sense of familiarity with her environment. Looking out of the window she saw a large old house, and as she looked she felt she had at one time lived in it. So familiar with it did she feel that she described the interior arrangement of the rooms and other details to her companion. Finding that the train would not move for some time, they left it and went to the house and asked permission to go through it. Everything was arranged just as described.

Subsequently, this lady came in touch with the doctrine of human reincarnation. On the strength of her experience she grasped the doctrine readily and lost no opportunity to tell her story as a verification of it, stoutly affirming she remembered living in the house in a previous incarnation. Finally, a friend took the trouble to look up the history of the section where the house was located, and found that it had been settled at a date much later than the lady's birth, and that there had been no houses in that section previous to a time when the lady who had the experience was full grown in the present life. Therefore, although familiar with the interior of the house, and feeling sure she had lived in it in a previous life, she could not have done so because the house was not there until long after her present birth.

I could fill a large volume with the experiences of those who feel certain they remember past lives, in which factors are present that when looked up historically have proved beyond any doubt that the experiences as described could not have taken place.

This remembering of past lives is on a par with reading the "akashic records." It is a similar experience and under the same laws. Therefore, without in any manner wishing to question the sincerity of either, but using them merely as examples with which to illustrate the utter fallibility of psychically received information when it has any bearing upon established religious conviction, I may be pardoned, I hope, for mentioning Dr. Rudolph Steiner and Mr. Leadbeater.

These two men, Dr. Steiner as the head of the Anthroposophical Society and Mr. Leadbeater as a Theosophical leader, together with a lady to be mentioned shortly, are perhaps the most influential exponents of the theory of human reincarnation in the world today. All three are believed by their followers to be gifted with wonderfully accurate psychic powers. Yet these very psychic powers, depended upon to verify the theory of human reincarnation, when actually put to a test which later came within the scope of historical verification failed miserably.

Dr. Steiner, reading the "akashic records" finds the discrepancy between the genealogies of Jesus as given in the gospels of Matthew and Luke is due to the fact that there was not one Jesus but two. The evidence, as summed up by the editor of *The Occult Review,* is:

> Surely the obvious and only tenable conclusion we can arrive at is that through some method or other the records of the Zohar found their way into Dr. Steiner's brain.

In other words, instead of the infallible reading of the "akashic records," Dr. Steiner was merely reading a tradition embodied in the Zohar, and probably having no basis whatever in fact.

Mr. Leadbeater, through his seership, was able to write the *Lives of Ulysses,* but it has turned out there is reliable historical evidence that his chronology is wrong, and ample evidence that the names he gives to his characters, instead of being read from the "akashic records," have been taken clairvoyantly or otherwise from a modern writer. In regard to him the editor of *The Occult Review* concludes:

> With the latter, however, there is the suggestion or suspicion of tinkering with earlier historical records and putting them in a new setting with a view to establishing or defending certain reincarnationist theories, with which history, by a violent abuse of chronological facts, is made to square. Here, of course, space does not permit of extensive comment, but the writer quoted is notably sympathetic both to human reincarnation and to Theosophy. For a full discussion of the reading of the ""akashic records" by Dr. Steiner and Mr. Leadbeater I must refer the reader to "Notes of the Month," and two articles, all appearing in *The Occult Review* for January, 1923 (Wm. Rider and Son, London).

I might go on to show how another Theosophical leader and world-renowned exponent of human reincarnation, for a long period claimed to remember she had been Cleopatra in a past reincarnation, but has lately decided she was not. I might take up, one by one, the statements of prominent persons regarding their past lives and give these statements the benefit of analysis. But not only is this too much like criticizing people, but I am convinced that in most cases they are quite sincere in their belief, and that this sincerity springs from actual psychic experiences which have been misinterpreted.

In the first place, due to astral substance inter-penetrating and surrounding all, retaining whatever vibrations are imparted to it, every idea ever held by man and every thought having passed through his mind, persist in the astral. All the world's events of the past have left their impress as vibrations in the astral substance associated with this earth. A person naturally sensitive, or one having cultivated the lucidic senses, who comes into rapport with the astral vibrations recording a past event sees that event as if it were taking place before his eyes. Just as a psychometrist upon touching a letter written by someone years before has all the thoughts and sensations that the person had while writing the letter, so a sensitive person who comes into rapport with an astral record feels as if he were actually witnessing or taking part in the recorded event.

Unfortunately for the infallibility of thus reading the "akashic records," there is always the human equation of the sensitive. Not only will any idea that is strongly dominant in the mind of the sensitive tend to warp the whole reading to support this idea, but a person in the subjective condition usually present while reading the "akashic records" is just in the right condition to be susceptible to suggestion. Just as a hypnotized subject, if told he is king, will carry out the impression to the smallest detail, thinking of a surprising number of things to make it realistic, so a sensitive, if given a single suggestion when in a subjective state, will weave about the central idea wonderful phantasies that all seem to bear a logical relation one to the other.

For instance, it is a common occurrence in our astrological classes, from which no one is barred, for some person in the audience, when a birth chart is placed on the blackboard, to commence telling all about the past life of the individual whose chart is up for discussion. If allowed to do so, half an hour will be consumed in telling the past lives in great detail, and just what events led up to the person being born with the kind of a horoscope he has. The whole thing is painted with a realism that is quite convincing. Now, one would think that a person psychic enough to relate so many details of past lives—about which no tests of accuracy can be made—would also be able to relate a few details about the present life. But when called upon to tell the events of the present life also, there is a strange silence, or else events are given that when the identity of the owner of the birth chart is made known can quickly be proved not to have taken place.

A person giving such a reading from a birth chart is under the influence of suggestion. He is dominated by a central idea—that of reincarnation—and for every discordant aspect he sees in the birth chart his imagination supplies him, quite vividly to be sure, with some sin in a past life. And if his fancy is still further freed under the influence of this self-applied suggestion, he will bring in elementals who are attached to the unfortunate, or the dweller on the threshold, and sundry other things that he feels have become associated with the victim in a past life.

There is also the person, growing in number and popularity, who without a horoscope or other guide than your presence, gives a dramatic recital of one or more of your past lives. Ask him what happened to you a thousand years ago and he will glibly tell you. Ask him what happened yesterday or a year ago and he cannot tell. These people are not dishonest. They believe what they say. But they are no more responsible than if hypnotized by a hypnotist and told by him that they could read the previous lives of persons. In the hypnotic state they would supply the information required whether it exists in actuality or not. As it is, they supply the information required because they have induced a self-hypnotic state while acquiring their lucidity, or psychic ability, and at the same time they have so strongly suggested human reincarnation to themselves while in this state that it has come to exercise a control over all their psychic perceptions; as much so as if the control had been brought about by the suggestion of a hypnotic operator.

But aside from these people who find it so easy to relate events of the past lives, and so difficult to discern those of the present one, there are others who have psychic experiences that are not due to self-hypnosis, yet usually are interpreted as proofs of human reincarnation. In the case related of the lady who felt she had lived in the house and was familiar with all its details, it is unlikely she had ever visited the place while out of her body in sleep. It is more probable that, becoming partially lucid, the condition of rapport was established between herself and the astral counterpart of the house. She really psychometrized the house, and no doubt, if she had tried she could thus have followed the astral record of the house back to the time it was built, and witnessed many scenes in its history. In a similar manner, a psychometrist upon touching a pebble is able to see and feel its history and relate it as if he had been an eye-witness to the geological changes that brought the pebble to its present form and station. He does this through his ability sympathetically to vibrate to the records persisting in the astral substance associated with the object. He feels as if he had been right there at the time the event transpired, and unless familiar with the laws governing psychometry might very well believe he actually witnessed the occurrence in a previous life.

In fact, it is quite natural to consider any psychic experience as an example of a revived memory. Things seen clairvoyantly or in sleep are not seen with the physical eyes, things heard clairaudiently are not heard with the physical ears, and things felt psychometrically are not felt with the physical sense of touch. They are perceived by the corresponding senses of the astral body. These perceptions are recognized by the unconscious mind, and may or may not rise up into the region of objective consciousness. In reality they exist in the unconscious mind precisely as does the memory of a physical experience. They are subject to all the laws of memory. To rise into objective consciousness there must be some association between the psychic experience and some thought already present in the objective mind, unless the person is in the subjective state as when hypnotized or under the control of a disembodied entity, in which case he is perceiving what the operator desires him to perceive. We do not remember past events except when there is a link between what is already present in the objective mind and what we remember. This link of association may be very slight, but it is none the less present. Neither is a psychic experience recognized to have taken place except there is a similar link of association between it and what is already present in the objective mind.

Unlike objective experiences, which are first recorded in objective consciousness and then imparting vibrations to the soul, reside there as memory, psychic experiences impart vibrations to the unconscious mind first. Later they may or may not, as the case may be, transmit motion to the physical brain in such a manner that the experiences are recognized objectively. If they do so, a psychic experience may be recognized almost at the instant it is experienced. On the other hand, the objective mind may be so occupied with other things that the experience resides in the unconscious a long time before there are lines of association between it and what is in the objective mind strong enough for it to be objectively recognized. But in any case, it first is memory. It is not to be wondered, then, that so frequently what is beheld or felt psychically should seem to be something remembered from the past.

I have spoken only of psychometry in connection with physical things. But there is another form of psychometry that is quite common. Every person who has lived and died has left the record of his experiences in the astral substance associated with this planet. Even as similar positions of the planets in the birth charts of two living persons tend, if the persons are brought together, to establish a close rapport between them, so persons who have lived and died leave a vibratory record in the astral substance that readily is attracted by a living person who has a similar birth chart. That is, by the law of resonance, one is very apt to attract and form the conditions of rapport with the astral record of a person who in life had a similar birth chart. Most persons, not being sensitive enough, are unconscious of such experiences. But one partially or wholly lucid, under these conditions will undergo a semi-transfer of identity, and will live in memory the experiences that the person whose record is thus contacted actually had. They are the actual experiences of a person who lived and died, but they are not the experiences of the psychic in a former life.

Further, the actual experiences of a person while out of the body during sleep reside as memories in the astral brain, and when some line of association is set up that causes some of them to be remembered they are often mistaken for experiences of a past life. During sleep, man's consciousness resides in the astral body, and it is quite common for the astral body to leave the physical body and travel to such regions as its strongest desires attract it to. Thus those interested in certain lines of thought may be attracted during sleep to schools in the astral world where these subjects are taught. Usually these experiences are not remembered on waking, or are greatly distorted in their transmission through the physical brain, although proper training will enable them to be brought back more completely. But in physical life, when confronted with some fact or doctrine or experience, there may be a sudden feeling that it has been encountered before, and that it is all quite familiar. This may be true, but it was not in a past life. It was encountered while out of the body in sleep, in this one. In fact, comparison with the known conditions of the world in the past frequently proves that the knowledge or experience with which one feels thus familiar without having contacted it physically in this life, could not possibly have been gained in a past life; for the factors involved are of too modern origin.

The facilities for movement and perception are so much greater on the astral plane, that people usually meet there before meeting on the physical plane. Of course, such meetings are seldom remembered on waking. Yet when two persons meet in the physical there may be a feeling they have met before, and it is quite easy to jump to the conclusion that there was friendship or enmity in a past life. As a matter of fact, which a little psychoanalysis will often reveal, they have actually met on the astral plane during sleep.

Geniuses and prodigies also are sometimes cited as indications of human reincarnation. But to one familiar with astrology the fact that they exhibit precocity or unusual ability cannot be related to previous human experiences of their own. They are related to previous human endeavors, it is true, but it is to those recorded in the astral substance surrounding the planet, and to disembodied human beings who have labored along the same lines. That this is the true interpretation, rather than the human reincarnation one, is evident in the fact that in the birth chart of genius those planetary positions are always most pronounced that indicate the ability to contact the inner plane, and draw directly from its records and its inhabitants.

In such cases the planet Neptune is always prominent in the chart, giving the sensitiveness of nervous organization that enables them to contact the vibrations from the astral world. This sensitiveness to the astral world gives rise to the temperamental idiosyncrasies of such people. In their highest work they enter into a state of abstraction that partly shuts from their mind the external world. Thus, although they may not be conscious of the source of their inspiration, they come directly into contact with that portion of the astral world, and with discarnate entities, which are sympathetic with the work in hand.

Aptitude for any branch of learning, whether genius is present or not, is indicated by the configurations of the planets in the birth chart. These configurations of the planets map the thought-cells in the astral form at birth. Such thought-cells have been formed by the experiences of the soul previous to birth in human form. They were formed because the original quality of the soul attracted it during the course of its evolution to these experiences, which are necessary to its development, that it may fulfill its own particular function in the cosmic structure. Because there is need of workmen of different types in universal construction, souls differ in original quality, and pass through different experiences. Some, like oaks, grow slowly and thrive in certain environments; others, like the fir, grow swiftly and rejoice in a different atmosphere.

All must admit that the first human incarnation was determined by the original quality of the soul, plus the various experiences which constituted its need for expression when born into human life. To account for the later difference in souls, it is necessary to assume they differed in their first incarnation either in character or in opportunity, or that it is but a matter of more numerous incarnations. If it is but a matter of more numerous incarnations that causes the difference between people, then we must believe all people are alike, except some are older than others, in which case both effort and karma become useless factors. But if people differed either in character or opportunity in their first human incarnation, then we have an example of a condition not caused by karma just such as karma was invented to explain. In any alternative, the introduction of the theory of karma is redundant.

Neither does heredity alone—the heredity genes of modern science—explain the diverse mental, moral, and physical qualities of children of the same parents. The thoughts and feelings of the parents at the moment of union have a great influence upon the quality of the soul then attracted. A child born from a love union is very different from one born from a union of the same parents in which one at the time was actuated by inflamed passion and the other was filled with loathing and disgust. Such differences in children, as well as the contributing factors, are revealed by their birth charts, but it has nothing whatever to do with human reincarnation.

Nor is the observation that certain types of intelligence and character recur at given intervals indicative of human reincarnation. One might as well say that all persons born between March 22nd and April 21st are reincarnated Romans, because they exhibit war-like tendencies.

At regular intervals certain planetary configurations recur. The most perfect of these cycles is called the Naros. Thus about every 600 years the sun, moon, and naked-eye planets occupy the same relative positions. It is possible, then, for persons to be born with birth charts practically the same as others who lived 600 years before. Of course, the plane from which the mental forces are received, ruled by the precessional cycle during which the equinox is about 2,156 years in each sign, and the avenue into which the efforts will be directed, ruled by planetary sections of about 308 years, will be different. But in a general way, it is quite possible for characters and history apparently to repeat. Yet, if the same players do appear time after time on the stage of life to act the same parts, they have failed to profit by former mistakes and are making no progress. They are going round and round, like squirrels in a cage, without getting anywhere. It is from this wheel of material rebirth that the Oriental devotee seeks to free himself and enter nirvana, another realm in which there is no progress, and, most pleasing to the Oriental mind, no effort.

But in all Nature, I defy anyone to point out one single instance of such stagnation. Eternal Progression is the anthem of creative life, applicable alike to material atoms, to human souls, to planets and starry systems, and to angelic hierarchies. All Nature moves in a spiral. The life-wave carries the soul irresistibly upward. It cannot stop, it cannot retrace its steps. Souls may appear to be going backward, even as planets appear to retrograde, but when viewed from a greater height, neither soul nor planet in reality is retrogressive. The utmost that might be accomplished toward thwarting Nature's purpose of eternal progression would be through defiance of her laws to bring about self-destruction. Such, according to an old tradition, is the fate of self-willed black magicians.

Nature's capacity is not so limited that she need force man back again to earth for experience. Nor need she pass all souls through the same experiences, nor give one soul the same experience again. Her resources are boundless, and she ever seeks variety in her expression. No two souls are being fitted for the same place in cosmic work, and as a consequence no two souls have exactly the same experience. To one who has the eye to see Nature about him, how clearly she strives for diversity!

Now there is a peculiar thing about those who believe they remember their former lives. Ninety-nine percent of them, at least, remember when they were celebrities of some sort. Apparently numerous incarnations have helped them not at all; for they are now mediocre. Indeed, they seem to have retrogressed.

I have met reincarnated Napoleons who knew nothing of military tactics. I have met great philosophers of the past who in the present life are confined in thought to the narrowest sectarianism. Those who were once high priests of Egypt, now know nothing of the ancient mysteries. An authoress of considerable note remembers when she was Mary Magdalene, but is quite ignorant of certain customs of the time, and in a later book expresses doubt if there ever was such a person as Jesus.

Another peculiar thing about these revived memories is that a soul in reincarnating seems capable of much division. The general favorites are: Napoleon, Joan of Arc, Daniel of lion den fame, and Alexander the Great. There are others almost as popular, but in almost any community of size where reincarnation is much taught, there will be found one or more of each of these. Several of each walk the streets of Los Angeles.

I believe there are two distinct reasons why usually, though not always, past incarnations that are remembered are those of important personages. The first reason is egotism combined with autosuggestion. In all of us is the latent desire to be heroic. We desire to be someone of note. In remembering past incarnations a person is in a psychic condition, and the unconscious desire to be someone great acts as a suggestion to the imagination, which fulfills the expectation by bringing into consciousness such apparent memories. The same factors operate in the case of the more ignorant and less progressive spirit mediums, who feel sure they are controlled only by great personages, or even by the Master Jesus Himself.

The other reason is that those who have been notable persons in the past have had potent minds or have lived strenuous lives, and thus have left a more powerful record in the astral substance surrounding the planet. The vibrations they have left are therefore more easily contacted, and it is quite natural that a person who is partially lucid should get into rapport with these astral records of notable persons and thus remember them, rather than that they should contact the records left by less potent people.

I have watched with considerable interest the kindly effort of reincarnationist friends to read my own past lives. On one occasion, when I had been studying Egyptian matters, and felt I had contacted Egyptian teachers, I was given much information concerning my Egyptian incarnations. On another occasion, after studying along an entirely different line, I was told of incarnations that seemed to dovetail with the nature of my researches. Other lines of thought on my part brought to light other incarnations. Except in Egyptian matters, in which they know there is a permanent interest, my friends were unaware on these occasions what I had been studying. Apart from the fact that some of these various incarnations overlap, thus making some of them at least impossible, I have reason to believe that my studies had attracted to me records, and also entities, and that these well intentioned friends had given me a psychometric reading of what I had attracted.

Having now, I trust, shown that the various evidences put forward as proof of human reincarnation are in reality misinterpretations of psychic phenomena and thus capable of a better explanation, it is time to inquire how and why the doctrine came to be so widely accepted. Certainly it is not an occult doctrine, for occult doctrines and esoteric teachings in the past were reserved for the initiated few. The seething masses were ever fed the husks of truth. And about human reincarnation there has been no secrecy at any time. It was proclaimed from the housetops. It is a sacerdotal dogma.

As such it was put forward by the priesthood of the Orient for the very same purpose that other dogmas have been foisted upon the public by the priesthood of the West.

This is not a tirade against the teaching of any great soul or Master, but merely a rehearsal of the usual fate of a truly spiritual doctrine. The teaching is given out by some inspired teacher as a message then most needful. It attracts a following and gains in impetus. But as its influence spreads it attracts to it a dominant priesthood, or is appropriated by the priesthood already in power. The priesthood have ever held it to be their prerogative to be the custodians of the mysteries. And for a time they may be unselfish in their enthusiasm. But the time comes when they or their descendants find the temporal power and advantage of their position is of greater importance to them than keeping their doctrines pure. Consequently, to keep in power and to obtain subservience from the masses, such dogmas are formulated and incorporated into their creeds as they think will best serve this end. Finally, the real spiritual ideas are lost to the priesthood, and the whole religious system becomes a machine to further their own material ambitions.

Of course, people under the yoke of oppression and surrounded by injustice, have a tendency to rebel. So it becomes the aim of the priesthood to formulate and teach some doctrine that will make the populace content in their misery.

One common device to this end is the teaching that the priest is the sole interpreter of the divine will, and that the ruling power—usually hand in glove with the priesthood—is appointed by Deity, and therefore to rebel against him is to rebel against Deity. In Japan, the Mikado is a direct descendant from the sun, and his word is the word of Deity. The chief hierophant of the Buddhist Church, the Taley Lama, is said to be a reincarnation of Buddha. He is, therefore, quite as infallible as the Pope in Rome. We in the West also have the divine right of kings to rule, and "the King can do no wrong." These doctrines when believed by the populace make it possible for king and priest to live in luxury, while the people live in abject poverty.

More potent still as a doctrine to keep the populace in subjugation, is the teaching that obedience to priest and ruling authority will bring rewards after death, and that rebellion against them, will bring after death punishment. The Japanese soldier fights fearlessly and dies willingly for his ruler, because he believes that such a death brings the greatest possible rewards in the "beyond." Moslemism carries this idea to its psychological climax. It pictures alluring females, pillage and rich plunder, ease and pleasure, for the brave soldier who gives his life for his faith—that his ruler may live in luxury and power. That which the ruler has in this life is promised as a reward after death to those who faithfully serve him here.

In Christendom there has been injected into one of the finest teachings ever given to man an element that appeals to the most selfish instincts. We have here, instead of the original many mansions in "my Father's home," a heaven of gold and power and music as a reward for those who obey priestly dictates. And for those who deny the priestly interpretation we have the burning pits of hell. But, in addition, we also have another dogma resting on no greater authority likewise than its appeal as a psychological factor. It is vicarious atonement. It is the alluring appeal used by confidence men the world over: to get something for nothing. "Believe and be saved," instead of "do and be saved."

In the West every step civilization has taken has been opposed by the priesthood. Realizing that every discovery of science is a blow to their power, for an enlightened people will not stand oppression, they have done their utmost to impede progress. Thus it is that even today many scientific facts are loudly denounced, because they conflict with religious dogmas. Death bed conversions still promise salvation; and still the priesthood reap a rich material reward from those who would buy their way into heaven.

Yet, for keeping a populace servile and preventing discontent and insurrection, no other doctrine ever formulated has been so successful as the dogma of karma and human reincarnation.

The Caste System is the natural and obvious result of a belief in human reincarnation. Thus it is said in reincarnation countries that woman incurs the penalty of being born into female form because of sins previously committed, otherwise she had been born a man. And to treat a woman with respect is to interfere with karma and consequently be in danger of creating bad karma for oneself. So strong is this feeling, that in some places a man will not rescue his mother from drowning if to do so he must touch her. Karma permits him to extend a pole to her if one be handy; otherwise, she must drown.

Those born in the highest caste are supposed to have lived extraordinarily good lives to be thus rewarded, and so have a right to lord it over the next lower caste. Those born in the lower castes are supposed to have committed grave offenses in past lives, and so merit all the misery they endure. Thus it would be as unjust to alleviate their suffering as it would be to permit a criminal to escape the sentence imposed on him by legal authority. Furthermore, the lower castes, believing their sufferings but their just dues, permit the upper castes to prey upon and oppress them; for to retaliate would make more evil karma.

Of course the priests, as sole interpreters of the Deific will, retain the authority to say just what actions incur good karma and just what actions incur evil karma. Consequently, by teaching that evil karma results from the actions they oppose, and that good karma results from the actions they commend, they have a lever by which they can cause the populace at all times to do their will.

It is true that ideas reincarnate. In this sense reincarnation is a fact; but human reincarnation is an inversion of this reality. The thought of some man of faith and vision is contacted by other men who carry out the original idea even though the one who first thought it has passed on. Great ideas thus reincarnate time after time. Further, a Hermetic tradition holds that there are certain exceptions that prove the rule. Still-born children and congenital idiots, it is taught, having actually never fully incarnated in human form, may reincarnate.

Karma, too, has an actual part to play in existence; but in a very different manner from that taught by human reincarnationists. These base their doctrine on two ideas that are fast becoming obsolete in all civilized countries. One is the old Jewish code of an eye for an eye and a tooth for a tooth. Criminal punishment, to be sure, up to the present time the world over, has been based largely upon vengeance. Because the criminal had violated a man-made code, it was proposed to make him suffer. A few hundred years ago in the most advanced countries even a petty theft was punished with long imprisonment or death. Later it was recognized that the punishment should be commensurate with the seriousness of the crime. And this seems to be the idea of the reincarnationists as applied to karma.

But it is fast coming to be recognized that people commit crimes, and that people sin, for one reason only, and that is through ignorance. Had the criminal a full realization of the manner in which his acts against society react on his own character, had he the vision to see the full consequence of his misdirected energy, he would commit no crime. In fact, crime more often than not arises from the entirely false notion that one person may truly gain at the expense of another. Otherwise it arises through lack of self control, which again is ignorance; the ignorance of how properly to control the thoughts and actions.

Society is beginning to recognize this, and as a result we hear less about punishment. The idea of vengeance, or even of payment to society for transgressions, is gradually being abandoned and in its place we hear more about reeducation. Instead of punishing criminals, of getting even with them, they are merely restrained, and this for the protection of society. When it is deemed they no longer are a menace to society, that they have been reeducated to a point where they will not endanger others, it is more and more the practice to parole or pardon them.

Neither do I find Nature seeking vengeance. Those who transgress her laws, it is true, suffer. But when they gain sufficient insight that they obey her laws, suffering no longer serves a purpose. Primitive man no doubt suffered with the cold, but when he learned how to start and maintain a fire his need to suffer with the cold was less; for he had learned how to adapt himself to an environmental influence. So also, now that man has arrived at the stage of his evolution where efforts for the welfare of others are the prime necessity for further progress, such efforts adapting him to present and future environmental influence, he needs no further punishment for transgression. Instead, he needs to be taught the advantage of working persistently for the advancement of all.

The other obsolete idea is that the important adjustments in Nature are the result of the intervention of superphysical intelligences. It was once thought that volcanoes only erupted when the god in the mountain was angry. And now we have the Lords of Karma who seem to be the administrators of karmic law, much as Jehovah was once envisioned on a throne meting out justice here and granting favors there.

There is, as I said, some truth in the idea of karma; for every act and every thought adds energy to the astral body, and these energies, both here and hereafter, determine the environment and events attracted. Furthermore, every act and every thought are recorded in the astral substance about the planet. At death the soul passes through this thought world of its own creation, faces these records, and passes judgment on its own acts. Unless it has built up, by a refined life and unselfish endeavor while still on earth, a dominant spiritual vibratory rate, it will be compelled, through the law of resonance, which supplants gravitation, to live on lower astral levels until by appropriate thoughts and acts it has spiritualized its dominant vibration. Then it will move to a higher inner-plane level. Karma, it will thus be seen, is really the influence of the thought-cells within the finer form as these have been organized by the mental attitude toward experiences. It has no power to force the human soul back to a life upon the earth.

Fearing that the truth about these things may be learned by the people, and thus upset priestly assumption to knowledge by revealing a conscious progressive life after death instead of either human reincarnation or a dreamy and purposeless nirvana, the priesthood of the East have endeavored to discourage investigation by formulating the doctrine of "shells," warning against elementaries, and attributing all communications from loved ones who have passed on to depraved earth-bound spirits. In the West, that their pretensions to knowledge might not be shown to rest on ignorance, the priest-hood have quite as strenuously opposed investigation of the life after physical death, attributing all communications from the "beyond" to devils.

As a further example of priestly machination, we learn from *The Inner Life*, by Leadbeater, that the head of the Eastern hierarchy is one of the few remaining Lords of the Flame who came down from Venus nearly eighteen million years ago, and that the two masters who inaugurated the T. S. will become the temporal as well as the spiritual leaders of the Sixth root race. It is plain what power would be placed in the hands of the priests, were these doctrines widely accepted. And from the effort made to pave the way I should not be surprised if an attempt soon were made to palm off on the West a fake avatar (this was written and published December, 1917).

For earnest Theosophical students the world over I have the utmost love and respect. But this Eastern hierarchy proclaims that the one thing that the West most needs is the teaching of reincarna-tion and karma. Yet such a belief devitalizes effort and causes social evils to be considered as just and inevitable. Instead, it seems to me, the West and East alike need the teaching that where man wills, the gods themselves are powerless. Inharmonies of some kind will exist as long as the planets form inharmonious aspects, but the discord need not manifest in its present manner. By wise education abolish the injustice of man to man, by wise attention to hygiene, dispose of sickness, do away with the evils of poverty and wealth, and Fate and Karma, aided by all the planets in the sky, are powerless to reproduce them. We need no teaching of servility to evil and injustice. What is needed is the teaching of man's divine birthright.

Heartsick, I have listened to professed teachers of occultism seriously inform their classes that owing to present world condi-tions, it would be impossible for them to develop their inner faculties in this life, and that all they could hope to do would be to try to bring back a consciousness in the next, that would spur them to such effort. What an incentive for souls after death to linger about the earth, bound to it by desire and the false hope of reincarnating! I have known promising occultists whose inner consciousness and soul faculties were already partly awakened, to be discouraged by such advice and cease making an effort. People come to our classroom in ill health, and boast they are making no effort to cure their infirmities, because to do so would be to interfere with their karma. And the one thing that causes us more correspondence than any other in the mail-order part of our work is the idea so many people have, that their hard lot in life is due to a just karma, and either that it is not worthwhile trying to change conditions, or that it would not be right to overcome their wretchedness. I know hundreds of people personally and through correspondence, whom the dogmas of karma and human reincarnation have unfitted for useful and efficient lives through inducing negativeness and stifling effort.

Here in the West we have made greater strides in civilization, because we have been able to free ourselves more fully from priestly dogmas. But in the East the dogmas of karma and human reincarnation have such a hold on the people that they have sunk into physical and mental apathy. The condition of the people where these dogmas are accepted proves this to be true.

I have shown, I believe, that all the so-called proofs of human reincarnation rest upon misinterpretations of psychic phenomena. I have indicated the source of its origin to be a crafty priesthood; who continue to use it as their most effective means of keeping in power and commanding servility from the populace.

It blights the hope of a conscious spiritual life by teaching that the earth is the only place where experience may be had, and that the ultimate haven is nirvana. This is essentially a materialistic doctrine, for it narrows the mind to earthly things. It makes universal brotherhood impossible because it teaches each is already receiving his just dues. Thus it quenches the unselfish impulses of the soul to assist others. The soul sinks in despair at the thought of innumerable births to come amid all the sordid surroundings of earthly life. It is a dogma that stifles initiative, makes for servility to tyrants, is materialistic, and in my opinion, the most pernicious doctrine ever accepted by a human mind.

Human reincarnation is an orthodox teaching of the Orient. Because of modern discoveries, no one any longer believes in the other ideas about Nature held by those who lived in the period when the orthodox beliefs of both East and West were formulated. The workings of God's Great Evolutionary Plan as observed in the operations of Nature, and the Universal Moral Code, are explained in Course 19, *Organic Alehemy.*

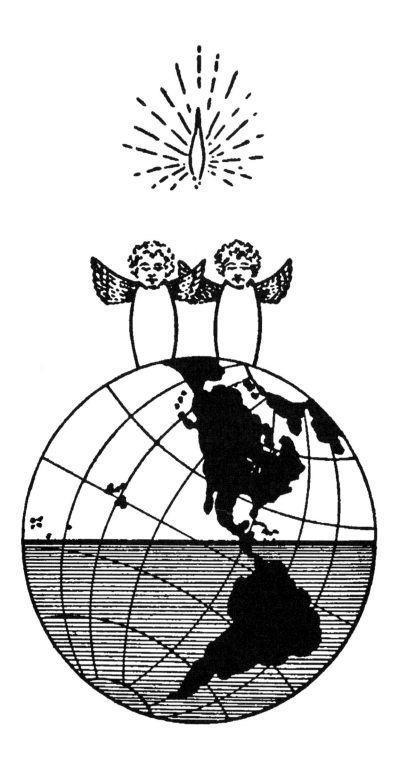

Chapter 9

The Ritual of
Egyptian Initiation

THE Western World is fast becoming aware that beneath the allegories and unconvincing verbiage of the sacred books there lies concealed a primitive secret doctrine, that behind apparently meaningless religious usages and pious jugglery there is a substance of sound psychological practice, that even outside the consecrated precincts of the Church—notably in Freemasonry and kindred fraternities—there are rites and ceremonies which convey by their symbolism fragments of knowledge concerning the history and destiny of the soul. Convinced of this, many worthy students are now endeavoring to raise the veil that so long has shrouded the mysteries of antiquity, hoping to solve the sacred allegories and correctly to interpret the symbolism of modern fraternities. To assist these in their research, I here propose to describe in detail the various steps, explaining the esoteric significance of each, of the ritual of initiation as conducted anciently in Egypt.

Not that the ceremonies and elaborate rites of the Samothracian Mysteries, those of Eleusis and Bacchus in Greece, and the Saturnalia of Rome, as well as the ritual of modern Freemasons, lack in mystical significance do I select Egypt, but because without exception these latter derived their procedure from the Mysteries of Ancient Egypt. Thus by interpreting these rites at their common source, even though they have been sometimes obscured by later transformations, we shall be able to perceive the fundamental concepts that underlie them all.

In this work we are fortunate in having a treatise, not entirely inaccessible to modern readers, that gives a detailed description of the Egyptian Mysteries. Iamblichus, a noted scholar and Neo-Platonist who lived in the first half of the fourth century, wrote a work upon the Egyptian Mysteries in which he portrays the principal steps and trials imposed upon the candidate during initiation. This description was translated into the French by P. Christian, and has been drawn upon freely for information by the more eminent students of the tarot, as it contains a complete description of the Egyptian tarot. In 1901 it was translated from French into English by my good friend Genevieve Stebbins, who has given me permission to make use of her translation in this lesson and in Course 6, *The Sacred Tarot*.

I, therefore, shall follow accurately the trials to which the Egyptian candidate for initiation was subjected, as described by Iamblichus, and shall endeavor at each step also to explain what originally was intended to be conveyed to the mind of the candidate. Such trials in some form, handed down from this remote period, persist today, as witnessed by the hazing of newcomers at school, and the riding of the goat in our lodges.

But why should tests of fitness for initiation be called riding the goat? This revolves about the significance of the five-pointed star which from antiquity has been employed as the symbol of man. The star placed with one point up has the significance of intelligence ruling the four elementary kingdoms, reason dominating the instincts of the flesh. It is thus the Grecian Hygeia, used by the Pythagoreans as the symbol of health. Now, in the zodiac the head of man, organ of intelligence, is ruled by Aries, pictured among the constellations as the Ram. In sacred works, consequently, to designate that the creative forces are directed by intelligence, it is common to refer to this circumstance as the lamb, and is so mentioned by St. John.

The five-pointed star when inverted, however, signifies man standing on his head; reason dominated by lust, passion, and selfishness; and is thus emblematical of chaos, the pit, black magic, and the devil. Zodiacally the home sign of Saturn, the origin of our Satan, is Capricorn, pictured in the firmament by a goat. The goat, whose beard forms the downward point, whose ears form the two lateral points and whose horns form the two upward points of a five-pointed star, therefore, as well as the inverted five-pointed star, is a symbol of black magic and evil. St. John refers to this inverted star as a falling star named wormwood. It will also now be apparent why the separation of the good and the evil should be referred to in the Scripture as dividing the sheep from the goats. The goat is the symbol of evil, and riding the goat signifies that temptations have been vanquished, the devil overcome, and the animal instincts sublimated into spiritual assets.

In the course of initiation, past or present, the candidate comes into the possession of new knowledge and new powers that alike are capable of either use or abuse, the proper application of which requires a high moral standard. To become master of the occult sciences, which ancient religious law forbade to be placed in writing, requires a strong intellect. The practice of white magic demands fortitude, persistence, self-confidence, and courage. Therefore, to prove the candidate's mental, moral, and physical fitness to receive the Hermetic Secret Doctrine, the strength of these qualities were, and are, subjected to test.

The primary object of all ancient Mysteries, however, and by far the most important use of the initiatory ritual, was to impress indelibly upon the mirror of his consciousness, by means of never-to-be-forgotten experiences, the past history, present opportunities, and future destiny of the soul. During the course of his travail there was also often another result attained. The stimulus received by his psychic faculties frequently opened the senses of the soul to visions of transcendental realms, and awakened the dormant powers of his divine self to new potency.

It is true that in some of the Mysteries the birth, crucifixion, interment, and resurrection of the sun were celebrated. But the initiate recognized in the sun's annual pilgrimage a direct analogy to the experiences of the soul in its cyclic journey. Likewise, in some, certain experiences of the soul were given preeminence. Thus the ecstatic reunion of the soul with its divine source gave rise to the Bacchic frenzies; the orgies originally representing the reunion of separated souls, the wine being emblematical of the mixture of masculine and feminine magnetism.

Now it is common knowledge that the classic nations, as well as other people of antiquity, believed in the doctrine that the soul once existed in a spiritual state of Edenic purity, was tempted to undergo involution into material form for the sake of experience, and must ultimately win its way back to paradisiacal bliss. While recognizing that sex symbols were a prominent feature in the Mysteries, and that sex doctrines were an important revelation, yet most commentors have preferred to omit them, either through ignorance of their true function, or for fear of shocking the modern sense of propriety. These sex doctrines of the ancient Mysteries are not what is currently termed sex practices, being neither devoted to sex magic nor to celibacy. They are doctrines of the true and pure relationship of marriage, such as today would be approved by our most eminent physicians and psychologists.

All life and activity being the result of polarity, the history and the mission of the soul can only be comprehended in association with its sexual activities. Now the ancient Secret Doctrine is very emphatic that in the beginning the ego is androgynous. After its differentiation, corresponding to birth, as it involves down from the celestial realm to the highest state of the spiritual world it develops a soul sphere—a sphere of consciousness organized in celestial substance. But to contact still coarser substance such as spiritual substance, astral substance, and physical substance, these energies become polarized into two separate channels of flow, into two organizations of consciousness, into two souls. This is the separation of the Twin Souls; who are over-shadowed and energized by one ego, yet each develops individual consciousness.

This separation is beautifully described in the Bible as Eve taken from the original Adam, who had been created in the image of God: "Male and Female created he them." Yet after the descent into material conditions and partaking of the evolutionary tree—gaining a knowledge of good and evil—to become as gods, as the Bible states it, they must also partake of the Tree of Life.

This tree of life is the reunion of the separated male and female souls. This is portrayed in the Greek ritual as Dionysus, slain and dismembered, after which the parts are collected and reunited in a new birth. In Egypt, Osiris is portrayed as murdered and the fourteen dismembered parts (each soul possessing a septenary constitution) sent floating down the Nile (the current of involutionary life) finally to be cast upon the muddy banks of the Delta (the material world). But faithful Isis (Nature) gathers together these fragments and breathing upon them the breath of life they become reunited and Osiris is born anew, never again to die. These allegories symbolically picture the drama of the soul's descent from the celestial state, the separation of twin souls in the highest realm of the spiritual world, who after a time Nature again brings together, breathes upon them the breath of love, uniting them, and by their united strength they become immortal.

Now, in the description of the trials with which Iamblichus has furnished us, the Sphinx of Gizeh served as the entrance to subterranean vaults in which the initiation was conducted. From between the forward limbs corridors closed by a secret door ran to crypts beneath the Great Pyramid.

As in modern fraternities, before the candidate was admitted to participate in the trials he must be selected by unanimous vote. Then he must give himself unreservedly into the hands of his guides and place implicit confidence in them, obeying their commands without asking questions. If we bear in mind that the whole ritual symbolically depicts the cycle of the soul, we perceive that this represents the faith that the soul should have in the wisdom and beneficence of Deity, and the obedience it should manifest to Nature's laws. The ego is called from an undifferentiated state by the unanimous demand for souls to be fitted for specific work in the cosmic scheme of things. During the earlier portion of their initiation into the mysteries of life, these souls do not know the why or wherefore of the suffering they endure; but if they place implicit faith in the guidance of their spiritual tendencies, at last they will see the light shine through the darkness, and following this, will be led into the glorious sunshine of Self-Conscious Immortality.

At a distance from the Sphinx the neophyte's eyes are bandaged, and he is led to its foot an unknown distance, where a door of bronze opens to admit him and then closes without noise. Bronze is an alloy of tin, ruled by Jupiter, and copper, ruled by Venus. Venus is the planet of love, and Jupiter in addition to being the planet of beneficence, through his rulership of the sign Sagittarius, the sign of the higher mind, is in one of his aspects considered the planet of wisdom. Bronze, therefore, represents not only a union of a male and a female potency, but also a fusion of love and wisdom. Now, the bandaged eyes of the neophyte represent the unconscious condition of the pure, diffusive spirit before its differentiation as an ego. The journey of the neophyte to the foot of the Sphinx represents the indrawing of this spirit potency to the celestial matrix of the ego's angelic parents. Its projection on the toilsome journey of involution and evolution, through the intense vibrations of wisdom and love of its angelic progenitors, is signified by the neophyte silently passing through the door of bronze.

The Sphinx, into which the neophyte enters, is a synthetic representation of all the energies in the zodiac, being composed in its unconventionalized form of the emblems of the four quadrants of the heavens—a lion, an eagle, a man, and a bull. It thus symbolizes a cycle, and because time is measured by the sun's passage through this cycle, it also signifies the passage of time. For the ego time was not prior to its differentiation.

Next, the neophyte is led down a spiral stairway of 22 steps and through a second bronze door which when closed so harmonizes with the wall of the circular chamber into which it opens as to be undetectable. He is halted upon the verge of an abyss and commanded to cross his arms upon his breast and remain motionless. In the heavens, the solstitial colure and the equinoctial colure make a cross, the original of the swastika cross. This heavenly cross, due to the revolution of the earth on its axis, apparently moves around the heavens each day from east to west, and due to the procession of the equinoxes moves through the constellations also from east to west, though slowly, and is thus symbolized by the swastika with its points turned to the left, this being the emblem of evolution. The swastika with its points turned to the right is the emblem of involution.

The spiral stairway of 22 steps symbolizes the involutionary descent through the embryonic celestial state of the seraphs, the door being the passage into the paradisiacal worlds of the cherubs, where for the first time vibrations of love and wisdom, represented by the door of bronze, begin to disturb the tranquil innocence of the ego. Twenty-two steps are emblematical of the zodiacal circle of 12 signs and the chain of 10 planets which exert their influence upon the soul, and upon all Nature, throughout all states, from the highest to the lowest. The soul's spiral pathway through each plane of existence is thus influenced by them. The candidate's crossed arms signify progress.

The candidate now halted upon the abyss, represents that state in which a rib was being removed from Adam for the creation of Eve. The abyss represents the grosser worlds into which the ego cannot descend; upon which it directly can have no influence. Its vibrations are too fine to affect substance coarser than that of the paradisiacal world, or upper realm of spirit, represented by the circular chamber in which the neophyte now stands. But during its descent through the seraphic realms it has evolved a soul sphere, or organization of consciousness, containing both male and female potencies. That it may transmit motion to grosser substance, this soul sphere polarizes its motion and divides into two organizations of consciousness, into two souls related to each other as male and female; the Adam and Eve of each deific ego.

While the candidate stands motionless upon the verge of the abyss, the two guardians who have accompanied him take from an altar, and dress in, white linen robes. One wears a girdle of silver and a mask representing the head of a bull, the other wears a belt of gold and a mask representing a lion's head. The robes of white symbolize purity, of linen, typify strength. Gold is sacred to the sun, and the lion's head is the sign Leo in which the sun exerts its greatest power. Silver is sacred to the moon, and the sign where the moon has its best influence is Taurus, symbolized by the head of the bull. Thus do the two guardians, in a most spectacular manner, represent the masculine and feminine portions of the ego's soul sphere.

The Thesmothete, as the guardian is called, representing Pi-Rhe, genius of the sun, stands at the neophyte's right, while the Thesmothete dressed as Pi-Ish, genius of the moon, stands at his left. Suddenly, with a great noise, a trap door descends in front of the neophyte, and at the same time the bandage is snatched from his eyes and he beholds the two figures, one on either side. Standing thus he represents the ego at the moment of parturition when the twin souls are born. The shock of their separation is denoted by the noise, and as Adam and Eve they stand by his side.

Then, from out of the abyss, only half of its body visible, rises a horrible mechanical spectre holding in its hands a huge scythe which, barely missing him, sweeps past the neophyte's neck seven times. This spectre is the symbol of death. The scythe represents the changes which time brings. Only the upper half of the spectre is visible, to designate that the higher qualities of the soul alone survive the changes of time. The seven sweeps of the scythe, weapon of death, indicate that the soul both in involution and in evolution passes through conditions ruled by each of the seven planets.

Now, according to kabalistical doctrine, before the creation of the universe there existed the all-diffusive spirit, called Ain Soph Aur. From this the universe came into manifestation by means of ten emanations, the first of which, called Kether, or crown, signifies motion, and corresponds in human affairs to the ego. The next two emanations are Chocmah and Binah, wisdom and intelligence, which involve the idea of polarity and correspond to the positive and negative souls at the moment of their separation. From this godhead, Kether, Chocmah, and Binah, the universe evolves by means of seven other emanations, or impulses; and according to the law of correspondences, the soul also builds its microcosmic universe about itself by similar means, the seven-fold constitution of man being evolved, as was indicated, by passing through environmental influences ruled by each of the seven planets, a circumstance symbolized by the seven sweeps of the death-dealing scythe, evolution being accomplished only after the separation of the souls, by means of successive lives and deaths.

After the enactment of this drama, the Thesmothetes lead the neophyte to the door of a small dark tunnel, giving him a lamp with which to light his way. The lamp represents the inner promptings of the ego which if listened to will direct the soul aright. He is now left to his own devices to indicate that the twin souls each go their separate ways. The tunnel is so small that to enter it he must proceed on hands and knees, and to indicate that once the cycle of necessity has been entered there is no return except through following out Nature's plan, the door immediately shuts behind him. This tunnel dips more and more downward as he follows it until finally it ends abruptly at the brink of a crater formed like an inverted cone. The tunnel symbolizes the descent of the soul through the spiritual realm, and the inverted cone, the sides of which are polished to reflect the light of his lamp even as in the astral world the astral light is seen, represents the astral world. Down the side of this cone he observes an iron ladder of 78 rungs, and finding no other method of advance open, he descends it. At the bottom of the ladder, he observes when he arrives there, a yawning well. Therefore, to find a way out he starts to ascend, looking carefully for a means of egress. Climbing seven steps upward he notices a crevice in the rocks just large enough to admit his body, and through this he squeezes, to find himself at the foot of an ascending spiral stairway.

The ladder is of iron to indicate that after leaving the spiritual realm the soul has entered a realm of force, a realm where animal tendencies as well as those higher are present, where the planet Mars has full sway. To indicate that during this period of its journey the soul is only a rudimental form, at no time can the neophyte assume the upright position, the position of the truly human. The 78 rungs of the astral ladder represent the influences that exert their power over the descending soul: the 12 zodiacal signs, the 10 planets, the 12 mundane houses and the denizens of the 4 astral kingdoms, the 36 decanates of the zodiac, and the 4 quadrants of the zodiacal circle.

The bottom rung of the ladder represents that point where the involving soul can go no lower, the point where it contacts the mineral realm and first incarnates in objective form. The 7 upward steps represent the 7 states of its evolution from mineral to man. In this seventh state the soul has behind it those experiences which have given it a complex astral organization, which enables it to be attracted to a human mother. The travail at its birth into human form is represented by the neophyte when he painfully squeezes through the narrow cleft in the rocks.

Now, from the beginning of its cyclic journey until it is born as a human being there are just 108 steps—22 prior to the separation of the male soul from the female soul, 78 involutionary steps through the astral realm, 7 steps from mineral to man, and an 8th step representing birth into the human form, symbolized by passing through the crevice in the rock. These 108 steps correspond to the 108 tablets of the more complete Egyptian tarot. The set of 78 cards commonly known constitute the exoteric set such as was revealed to all who succeeded in passing the trials here described. But initiates know that at an advanced stage, after undergoing soul purification, and being admitted to the rites of the inner sanctuary, the neophyte was instructed in the use of an esoteric set, consisting of 22 Astro-Masonic symbols, and that at a still higher point in initiation there was revealed to him a septenary of Kabalistical Pictographs, sealed with an 8th, thus constituting in all 108 tablets, completing the Deific number 9 (1+8=9).

Now, for all ordinary purposes the exoteric set of 78 tablets, which constitutes the common Egyptian tarot, is quite adequate. These are reproduced in Brotherhood of Light tarot cards. And here also, I believe, I should designate where the tablets of the esoteric set are accurately described. In ancient times these were kept most secret, but that they might not be lost to coming generations, they have been fully described and commented on in a book unfortunately now out of print, but which is possessed by many students throughout the world. This book is *Light of Egypt*, Vol. No. II, by T.H. Burgoyne. It presents this ancient esoteric set under the caption THE TABLETS OF AETH. The first 22 are the Astro-Masonic symbols referred to. Next is given a vision of the 10 great kabalistical powers, or angels, of the universe. The first 7 of these, as given under, VISION, are the 7 Kabalistical Pictographs referred to. But that this esoteric set may also be used separately as explanatory both of the kabala and of the 33 degrees of Freemasonry, there is added an eighth, ninth, and tenth pictograph, which were not included in the complete Egyptian set of 108 tablets. The seal, which is the seal of the earth, however, is given, a seal that is dual yet is one, the obverse and reverse view being represented on one tablet.

After the neophyte has passed through the cleft, symbolizing his expulsion into the world of human activities through the sacred yoni, he ascends the spiral stairway of 22 steps and halts before the entrance to the sanctuary. These 22 steps, symbolical of the influence

upon human life of the 12 signs and 10 planets, signify his experiences under their influence from birth to the time that he seeks occult
initiation. A grating of bronze—symbol of love and wisdom—bars
his progress, but a magus, called a Pastophore, opens the gate and
welcomes him in. Thus always is there a master ready to assist and
instruct the neophyte who, in love and in devotion to sacred science,
has successfully passed the early ordeals.

The neophyte now finds himself in a long gallery sustained by
sculptured caryatides representing 24 sphinxes, 12 on either side. In
each space between two sphinxes the wall is covered with a frescoed
painting, these 22 pictures being lighted by a line of 11 lamps that
extends between the two rows of figures.

A sphinx, representing the four quadrants of heaven, symbolizes
any cycle of time, and as here arranged they designate the 24 hours
of the day, as well as the 24 elders of the Apocalypse. The 22 frescoed
paintings picture the 22 Major Arcana of the tarot, the symbolism of
which at this time is explained to the neophyte and by him committed to memory. The eleven lamps are crystal sphinxes in each of
which burns an asbestos wick at the surface of a sacred oil, each lamp
being supported by a bronze tripod.

The flame of the lamp represents the ego, a living, brilliant,
changeless spark of Deity. The asbestos wick which ever feeds the
flame yet is never consumed, represents the immortal soul feeding
the ego with the results of its experiences. These experiences, gained
through cycles of time as symbolized by the form of the sphinx, and
in objective realms as indicated by the crystalline structure of the
lamp, are typified by the oil. The transparent quality of the lamp
suggests that matter offers no barrier to the sight of the initiate. The
tripod, upon which the lamp rests, an alloy of a positive and a
negative metal, presents the symbolic aspect of two interlaced trines.
The negative trine symbolizes involution, and the positive trine
evolution, together constituting the support of the soul and making
possible its conscious immortal existence.

One of the lamps is set slightly apart from the other ten and
represents the final synthesis of the others, symbolizing also the
point from which the neophyte departs to undergo further perils.
The 22 frescoed pictures each correspond to one of the 12 zodiacal
signs or 10 planets and constitute an esoteric interpretation of their
attributes and functions. The 22nd picture corresponds to the unknown; but each of the other 21 correspond either to one of man's
seven physical senses, to one of his seven psychic senses, or to one

section of his seven-fold constitution. Each is also related to one of the 21 branches of occult science that the neophyte is called upon to master before he can aspire to adeptship. Taken as a whole—as shown in detail in Course 6, *The Sacred Tarot*—they constitute a science of the will and an absolute religious doctrine, and each corresponds to a definite step in the neophyte's occult advancement. The 10 lamps represent the numerical decade as well as the ten emanations of the Sephiroth of the Kabala, and together with the 22 pictured Major Arcana point to the 32 paths of wisdom. With the final lamp, or 33rd symbol, they constitute the exoteric view of the same set of universal principles the esoteric side of which is set forth in the 33 TABLETS OF AETH previously mentioned. They, therefore, represent the original ideas from which the 33 chapters of the kabalistical book, Sephir Yetzirah, and the 33 degrees of modern Freemasonry, were derived.

The neophyte is permitted to remain in this Gallery of the Arcanum under the instruction of his master until he has thoroughly familiarized himself with all the symbols and their interpretations. This symbolizes all that he may hope to attain from the physical world.

To progress farther on the path, the soul must temporarily leave the physical world and soar into other realms where ascended souls will conduct its initiation on the inner planes. To reach the spiritual plane, either while still connected with the physical body or after death, the soul must pass through the four kingdoms of the astral world. To symbolize this journey, the neophyte leaves the Gallery of the Arcana. First, to represent his travel through the realm of the gnomes he passes through a tunnel. At the end of this tunnel, to represent the realm of salamanders, he is confronted with a roaring fire through which he must go if he would not retreat. This fire is really not so great as it at first appears, and he passes through it without injury, but no sooner has he passed it than it is replenished by unseen hands to make his return impossible. Thus he realizes an important truth; that in occultism he who places his hand to the plow and then turns back is lost. Next, as representing the influence of the undines, he is compelled to wade through a stagnant lake the water of which rises to his chin, but by going on tiptoe he manages to reach the opposite shore, and climbs dripping and cold upon a platform which he sees in front of a closed door.

This door is of bronze, and is divided laterally by a column on which is sculptured the head of a lion having in its mouth a ring figuring a serpent biting its own tail. The ring in the form of a serpent symbolizes eternity, and the lion symbolizes courage. Courage, therefore, he is made aware, should sustain his efforts throughout eternity. To open the door he grasps the ring, and as it resists he uses both hands. But no sooner does he get a firm grip upon it than the platform beneath his feet drops from under him and leaves him suspended in air, in the realm of the sylphs. The trap beneath his feet rises again promptly, and he passes through the door which now opens to permit his entrance. This bronze door symbolizes love and wisdom. It is divided into a right, or positive, half, and a left, or negative, half; the dividing column, placed where positive and negative forces join, symbolizing the tree of life that confers immortality. The sign Leo is natural ruler of love affairs. The lion's head, however, as Leo is ruled by the sun, also typifies the male element, while the circle in its mouth typifies the female element. The symbol as a whole, therefore, represents the complete and harmonious fusion of the sexes, actuated by love. Thus is conveyed to the neophyte's mind the thought that the door of the sanctuary opens only in the union of two harmonious souls inspired by love and guided by wisdom. Not by one alone can the spiritual heights be scaled, but through the mighty movement within the finer substances of space caused by the soul union of both.

The neophyte thus having triumphed over the tests by earth, fire, water, and air, representing his passage through the astral kingdoms, is now met by 12 Necores. These men typify the translated souls of those who once lived upon the earth and who belong to each of the 12 zodiacal signs. They blindfold his eyes, to signify the dullness of the real spiritual perceptions until higher initiation is attained, and lead him to a crypt beneath the pyramid where the college of the magi awaits him. This crypt symbolizes the spiritual world which he now ritualistically has entered. The pyramid above is a symbol of the earth which he has abandoned, and being directly above this crypt indicates the exact correspondence between the physical world and the world spiritual, between that which is above and that which is below.

The walls of this crypt are sculptured with the pictures of the 48 constellations that represent the influence and spiritual significance of the 12 zodiacal signs and the 36 zodiacal decanates. There are also pictured representations of the 7 planetary angels, and the 360 genii of the degrees of the zodiac, through which the sun passes in one year. Beneath each of these pictures is an explanation which can only be read by those possessing the key, this key being that of Spiritual Astrology, which is treated in complete detail in Course 7, *Spiritual Astrology*. At each of the four angles of the crypt stands a bronze statue posed upon a triangular column, one having the head of a man, one the head of a bull, one the head of a lion, and one the head of an eagle. These figures denote—as each is posed on a trine—the four zodiacal triplicities. Each head bears a cross—symbol of union of forces and of earth—upon which is a light, as if engendered by the union and representing the divine fire that permeates and vivifies earth.

The dome of the vault contains a golden rose of five petals. The rose, because it is harbinger of spring, represents renewed life. Five is the number of man, and gold is the metal sacred to spirit. This entire symbol represents those who have attained spiritual regeneration. From the rose are suspended seven lamps, each having three branches. The three branches signify the three great divisions of occultism: astrology, alchemy, and magic. Each of these is divided into 7 distinct subjects, the 21 branches signifying the 21 branches of occult science which the neophyte is called upon to master and which illuminate the mind of the adept.

Below this rose sits the Hierophant. He is dressed in purple, sacred to Jupiter, the planet governing the higher mind, indicating that he is master of the sacred sciences. His forehead is girt with a circle of gold to indicate that his mind is fully cognizant of spiritual things. From this band arise seven stars, indicating that he is in possession of the seven states of consciousness that are the heritage of the perfect man. He occupies a silver throne. This metal is sacred to woman, and indicates that he is not ignorant of woman's share in the attainment of spiritual victory. The throne is placed upon a raised platform, and thus indicates the exalted position which his knowledge and efforts have conferred upon him.

To indicate their purity, the other Magi are dressed in white. And to indicate that they also have the spiritual light, there is a band of gold about each brow. At right and left of the Hierophant they are arranged in triple semicircles, there being three semicircles on the Hierophant's right and three on his left, so that he occupies the central, or seventh, point between the two triads. The triad on the left is negative, and represents an equal development of body, intellect, and soul in woman. The triad on the right is positive, and represents an equal development of body, intellect, and soul in man. Thus the Hierophant, himself masculine yet occupying a throne of silver, by his unique position symbolizes the meeting and blending of the very highest type of man and woman.

In the rear, under a purple canopy, symbolical of beneficent Nature as she overshadows all, is a colossal statue of Isis. It is composed of an alloy of lead, tin, iron, gold, copper, mercury, and silver; each being a metal ruled by one of the seven planets and thus symbolizing one of the seven active principles that pervade all nature. The statue wears a triangular diadem of silver, with an aigrette of 12 rays, and upon her breast is a golden rose in the centre of a golden cross. The arms are extended in front in such a manner as to form an equilateral triangle with the forehead at the apex. From each of the open fingers streams toward the earth a golden ray.

The rose upon the golden cross symbolizes the united transmutation of positive and negative energies from a lower range of action to a higher scale of vibration. The ten golden rays typify the chain of ten planets through which Nature molds the destiny of all things. The silver aigrette of 12 rays represents the 12 zodiacal signs that act as sounding boards from which the vibrations of the planets are reverberated. The equilateral triangle of silver signifies woman who has proportionally developed her body, intellect and soul. The triangle from which flow the golden rays indicates man who has cultivated in a harmonious manner his body, intellect and soul. Thus their point at the top of the forehead of Isis denotes that Nature's crowning glory is the reunion of two such perfectly developed people.

Before the Hierophant is a table upon which rests a planisphere, and it is here, before the assembled college, that the neophyte, whose eyes are now unbandaged, is required to demonstrate his knowledge of astrology by erecting and delineating a birth chart, calculating the progressed positions and passing judgment upon the events that have taken place in some person's life, and the times when these events have taken place. In order to check the accuracy of his delineations, the chart of some person known to members of the college is selected, but its identity is kept secret from the neophyte. He is expected to portray the temperament of the person, to select the channels of activity into which the life has chiefly been turned, to designate what departments of life are fortunate and what are unfortunate, and to select the times and natures of the principal events that have transpired in his life. Also he is expected to know something of all the other six branches of astrology.

After his knowledge of astrology has been thoroughly tested, he is required to demonstrate his knowledge of the tarot. He must be familiar with the meaning of each of the Major Arcana in each of the three worlds as well as the divinatory significance. He must know the vibratory influence of names, numbers, colors, tones and flowers, and must have some knowledge of the talismanic properties of gems. And he must know how a particular name, number, or other vibratory influence will affect a certain person, as revealed by comparing it with the birth chart. Finally, he is required to lay out and correctly read a tarot spread, thus demonstrating his ability to use these tablets as divinatory instruments.

After these tests of his knowledge, he is required to take an oath, similar in its wording to that administered in modern Freemasonry, never to reveal the sacred sciences or other portions of the mysteries. Then he is required to take a second oath, vowing himself to submission and obedience to the Hierophant. This second oath represents the pledge the initiate makes to himself to obey always the voice of his conscience. At this point a terrible noise is heard and an artificial tempest is produced during which the Magi point their swords at his breast and accuse him of past crimes, typifying the day of judgment when the soul will be called upon to render an account of its deeds done while in the flesh. Next, two Necores, each carrying a cup of wine, approach and offer the cups to him. Then the startled candidate is told that one of the cups is quite harmless but that the other contains a deadly poison. Reminding him of the oath he has just taken to obey, the Hierophant commands the neophyte to make a choice of, and immediately to drink, the contents of one of the cups.

The harmless cup symbolizes love and virtue; the poison cup, passion and vice. Each soul is confronted with the trial of this choice, and only by obeying the Voice of the Silence can it safely be passed. If, in spite of his oath of submission, the neophyte refuses to obey, he is informed that the initiation is broken and he is confined to a dungeon for seven months and then allowed a second trial. If he thus fails at the first test he may never rise higher in the ranks of the Magi, though he may gain freedom later by successfully passing the test. In such a case he represents a weak and wavering soul who fears to obey the dictates of his inner self. The neophyte's only hope of escaping extinction is to pass the ordeal, though once failing he does not have the opportunities that would have been open to him had he taken the decisive step at once. The laws of the Magi compel him to pass the trial or perish in the dungeon cell.

Thus the soul, by virtue of moral integrity and aspiration, is represented as triumphing over the barriers that confine it to lower spiritual states. His blindfolded entrance to the crypt indicates his entrance into the first state of the spiritual world; the tests of his astrological and his kabalistical skill take him symbolically into the second spiritual state; his first oath conducts him into the third spiritual state; his second oath leads him into the fourth spiritual state; the trial of the cups gives him entrance into the fifth spiritual state; and now, to represent the sixth spiritual state, he is led into a neighboring hall which is furnished luxuriously to convey the impression of a royal nuptial chamber.

His clothing is removed by attendants, indicating that all grossness has been purged away. He is dressed in white linen to symbolize the strength of purity. An exquisite repast is enjoyed while his ears are refreshed by strains of rapturous music, emblematical of the higher states of ecstacy and the music of the spheres. As he finishes the refreshments, curtains are drawn aside, revealing to him beautiful young women dancing. To conceal their identity, even as the body hides the soul, they wear masks attached at the brow by a circle of gold, typical of intellectual illumination. They are scantily clad in a gauzy veil spangled with golden bees, the veil indicating how slight is the obstruction that bars man from realization, and the golden bees signifying the divine creative essence in its most spiritual aspect, and further, that the veil may be penetrated only by the industrious; for the slothful soul will never penetrate the spiritual states. Across each girl's shoulders is thrown a filmy scarf, symbolizing the spiritual raiment formed by exalted aspiration and devotion to truth; and each carries a garland of flowers, indicative of innocence, joy and supreme happiness.

Delightful perfumes fill the air, and the neophyte approaches the dancers. After a time two of their number throw their garlands about him, encircling him with a chain of roses, while the others flee. These two girls continue to dance about him, shaking their garlands by turn as if to provoke his choice. The chain of roses represents the binding power of love.

If the neophyte dares to violate the sanctity of the mysteries he is in actual danger, but if he continues to conduct himself with propriety the Magi come to congratulate him upon passing the last of the trials, and confer upon him the title of Zelator. This final act in the initiation symbolizes the reunion of twin souls, which takes place upon the boundary of the sixth and seventh spiritual states. While conveying the idea that all passion must be evolved upward into pure unsullied love before this state can be reached, and that this sacred union must not be profaned with violence or carnal desire, it at the same time, by the two girls dancing about the neophyte, symbolizes the original trinity that existed before the separation of the sexes—ego, male soul, and female soul. It should be noticed that this scene is very different from that representing the separation; for that was a region of hideous monsters and dim consciousness; while this is a place of joyous beauty, ecstatic sensations, and vivid perceptions. By this union the soul is represented as passing into the seventh spiritual state together with its long missing mate, and can no longer be considered human, for it has now attained to the state of angelhood; immortality is no longer a possibility, but an assured fact.

Lastly, to impress upon the new Zelator the fate of those who follow the inversive path, he is led in the midst of 12 Necores, representing the zodiacal signs, into the opening of a cavern. Here a pale, uncertain light reveals to him a pit in which a sphinx is tearing the effigy of a human form. So, according to tradition, will the cycles surely destroy those who lose their immortality by following the fateful road of selfishness and black magic. Thus ends the ritual of Egyptian initiation, portraying, as it does, the cycle of the soul.

Study Questions _____

Chapter 1, **The Two Keys**

1. By what means alone can nature's sanctuary be unlocked?
2. What was the prevalent condition of science prior to the 17th century?
3. What man refuted the old authorities, stating, "Nothing can be proved or disproved by unproved principles?"
4. By the aid of what can all sophisms be avoided and all problems solved?
5. What conditions prevent the soul from accurately conveying the truth perceived psychically to the objective consciousness?
6. What are the most valuable possessions used in arriving at the mathematics of truth?
7. What was the earliest form of worship?
8. What was the source of fire worship and sex worship?
9. What is the written law? What is the Golden Key to its interpretation?
10. What is the key to the door of positive knowledge?
11. What knowledge enabled Paracelsus to effect wonderful cures?
12. In what manner did the sacred books have their origin?
13. What is the Oral Law? What is the Silver Key to its interpretation?
14. What book had been consulted by the most learned kabalists and mystics?
15. To what do the twenty-two major arcana and the forty minor arcana of the tarot correspond?
16. To what do the court cards of the tarot correspond?
17. What is the relation of the Tarot to Astrology?
18. What is meant by the eclipse of the sun at the death of Moses?

19. What is meant by the moon being diminished at the death of David?
20. What relation had the Ark of Covenant to the Book of Thoth?
21. What symbolical representations were carried in the ark?
22. What are letters?
23. What are absolute ideas?
24. What are numbers?
25. Due to what fact are the Golden and Silver Keys of such great value?

Chapter 2, **The Zodiac**

1. Why can there be no intelligent study of occultism that omits astrology?
2. Define the Zodiac.
3. To what do the signs of the zodiac owe their peculiar influence?
4. What influence have the signs of the zodiac over the planets found in them?
5. Why does each sign transmit certain tones much more readily than other tones?
6. What sign in a birth chart indicates, in a large measure, the individuality?
7. What is the characteristic quality of people born under each zodiacal triplicity?
8. What are the four chief ways in which the zodiacal signs may be considered?
9. How is sight an apprehension of a trinity?
10. Name the signs belonging to each of the three Qualities, and state to what condition of matter each corresponds.
11. What is the meaning of Degree of Emanation?
12. Name the masculine signs of the zodiac.
13. What natural phenomenon does the sign of Aries resemble?
14. To what portion of the human anatomy does the sign of Taurus belong?
15. People of what sign are looking for the "why" of things?
16. To what degree of emanation does the sign of Cancer belong?
17. How are Leo people like, and how unlike, Aries people?
18. People of what sign are ever looking "how" desired results may be attained?
19. People of what sign are inordinately fond of approbation?

20. What is the dominant idea of Scorpio people?
21. What zodiacal sign rules the hips and thighs?
22. People of what sign are very diplomatic?
23. What airy sign possesses the most continuity?
24. People of what sign often lack self-confidence and are prone to worry?
25. Which sign has the most extremes of temperament and ability?

Chapter 3, **Mundane Houses**

1. What are Mundane Houses?
2. What is a House Cusp?
3. Where is the First House of a horoscope located?
4. Why is the top of a horoscope considered as the South? What houses are in the following, and what do they rule?
5. Trinity of Life.
6. Trinity of Psychism.
7. Trinity of Wealth.
8. Trinity of Association.
9. Which houses are Angular?
10. In which houses do the planets have the strongest volume?
11. Which are the Personal Houses, the Companionship Houses, and the Public Houses?
12. What houses are positive? Which tend toward increase? Name the following planets:
13. Vital Planets. Intellectual Planets.
14. Social Planets. Business Planets.
15. Harmonious Planets. Discordant Planets.
16. What planet rules the heart or vital center of life?
17. What planet has dominion over the animal appetites and passions?
18. What part of the human anatomy does Jupiter rule?
19. What is the octave expression of Mercury, of Venus, and of the Moon?
20. Which planet rules the astral body?
21. Give the one word that best expresses the nature of each of the planets.
22. What aspect has the nature of Venus?
23. What aspect has the nature of Mars?
24. What aspect is harmonious in the highest degree? Discordant in

the highest degree?

25. Give the one word that best expresses the nature of each of the ten aspects.

Chapter 4, **The Mission of the Soul**

1. What is the primary requisite for success in any enterprise?
2. Define ego.
3. Define the soul.
4. Did the ego ever have a beginning, and can it have an end?
5. Did the soul have a beginning, and does it change?
6. Why must the ego either remain unconscious or gain experience through contact with relative conditions?
7. What is the dual function that the soul develops?
8. For what purpose did the soul develop the power to mold forms?
9. How do the experiences of the soul in one form enable it to attract and mold a form of still higher organization?
10. Why could there be no love without experiences with relative conditions?
11. Why could there be no life without the experiences of functioning through forms in some kind of substance?
12. What is the answer to the question as to why we are here?
13. Why is contrast in experience to be desired?
14. Why is variety of experiences to be desired?
15. Why do the innumerable forms of the physical, astral, and spiritual worlds offer the best opportunity we can imagine for developing not only wisdom, but also love?
16. What are the two essential factors of immortal life?
17. Why is the cycle of the soul called the Cycle of Necessity?
18. What is the mission of the soul?
19. What is the process by which the soul evolves from the mineral state to incarnate as man?
20. What is symbolized by the Bible story of Eve being tempted and partaking of the forbidden fruit?
21. What is the relation of adaptation to immortality?
22. If man is to survive on the spiritual plane what must he have the power to do?
23. What is the general plan by which Self-Conscious Immortality may be attained?
24. What is the greatest wisdom?

25. What is the expression of the highest love?

Chapter 5, **Physiology and Correspondence**

1. Why is it illogical to think that a man is ever incarnated in woman's form?
2. When velocities are attained greater than that of light what happens to space, time and gravitation?
3. In the astral body what corresponds to the physical cells and structures of the physical body?
4. In what manner do states of consciousness perform for the astral body functions similar to those performed by sunlight for the vegetable world?
5. Why must man have food on the spiritual plane?
6. Why do some thoughts have an influence upon the astral body but not upon the spiritual body?
7. What enables energy derived from the motive Contribute Your Utmost to Universal Welfare to build the spiritual form?
8. In the maturation of the seed, to what event in human life does casting off of the first polar body correspond?
9. Name the ten realms in the Cycle of Necessity through which the soul passes.
10. In the adjustment of mankind to the Aquarian Age, what does the tenth and final step indicate?
11. What is of paramount importance to the individual?
12. What primarily determines the behavior of the individual and the events which enter his life?
13. Why, to be free from want and free from fear, and to possess freedom of expression and freedom of worship, should men be familiar with the facts of astrology?
14. Why are illiteracy, poverty, disease, heartrending toil and the acceptance of the doctrine of atheistic materialism hindrances to the development of spirituality?
15. Upon what must people chiefly rely for personal experiences that prove there is a Supreme Guiding Intelligence, and life after physical death?
16. What is the most destructive of all emotions, and how may it be banished?
17. Why are induced emotions so important?
18. Why does atheistic materialism strive to suppress the facts of

astrology and the facts of extrasensory perception?

19. Why should men be free to express their individual aptitudes?
20. The thought energies flow into and tend to develop what?
21. Why for true progress is it essential that man should be at liberty to change his religious views to conform to new information?
22. What are the nine points of the Nine-Point Plan for the New Civilization?
23. To what plane do the Four Freedoms set forth in association with the negative, or even, numbers, 2, 4, 6 and 8 chiefly relate?
24. To what plane do the Four Orders of Facts set forth in association with the positive, or odd, numbers, 1, 3, 5 and 7 chiefly relate?
25. Of the points in the Nine-Point Plan for the New Civilization, which is the most important?

Chapter 6, **Doctrine of Signatures**

1. What does the Solar Ray contain?
2. From whence are all the life-entities of our universe issued? To what do they correspond?
3. What law forbids the beginning or destruction of egos?
4. What constitutes Character of Genius?
5. How does the State of Life affect a soul?
6. What is meant by Degree of Emanation?
7. Describe the motives and impulses of a soul belonging to each of the four States of Life.
8. Describe the actions of a soul belonging to each of the three Degrees of Emanation.
9. What three factors determine the Doctrine of Signatures?
10. After differentiation, how is the soul affected by the states it passes through?
11. Is the Doctrine of Signatures confined to entities?
12. Do all peppers have their origin in the same Spiritual State of Life?
13. By what sign are the Irish people ruled?
14. Do things ruled by the same zodiacal sign harmonize?
15. What do the terms good and evil imply in relation to some definite entity?
16. How can we understand the manner in which man is influenced by objects in his immediate environment?
17. What birth chart position denotes the Planetary Family to which

a soul belongs?

18. By what Law do energy-centers in the astral form attract events of the corresponding quality?
19. What three distinct factors can change the energy centers mapped by the birth chart?
20. What happens to our astral bodies when we come in close contact with another person?
21. What does a comparison of birth charts indicate?
22. What is the first astrological consideration in a question of harmonious marriage?
23. Is there good ground for companionship between people belonging to the same Planetary Family?
24. What things indicate the strongest natural source of wealth?
25. How can the practical application of the Doctrine of Signatures help man?

Chapter 7, **Facts and Fancies About Reincarnation - 1**

1. Why is it dangerous to permit any idea to become so strongly entrenched that no one is permitted to criticize it?
2. Give the range of the number of human incarnations as taught by various schools.
3. What does human reincarnation imply?
4. What did Madame Blavatsky teach regarding human reincarnation while working under Western Initiates?
5. Did Madame Blavatsky teach human reincarnation before removing her headquarters to India?
6. Why is popular opinion a poor criterion of Truth?
7. What relation to progress are hardships, trials and sorrows?
8. Do events in themselves have a value, or can all events be made to create values for the soul?
9. What determines the value of any event of life?
10. Are there other spheres than the physical that offer every facility for progress?
11. Why is it difficult for many to think of any place of reward or punishment or progress other than earth?
12. What is the true cause of the apparent inequalities of life?
13. Is it logical to think the spiritual giants who have suffered have done so in punishment for crimes of previous lives?
14. Are all souls progressing to fulfill the same destiny?

15. Why are the educational needs of souls arriving at the human stage very different?
16. Is it probable that it requires many incarnations as a horse to produce a race horse, or many incarnations as a man to produce a college professor?
17. Why does the average savage have as much opportunity for spiritual progress as the common civilized man?
18. What opportunities for progress have those who die young?
19. If characters were equal and opportunities were equal would there be apparent inequalities in life?
20. Explain the justice of differences in character.
21. Can we say that human suffering is due to karma only, and disregard the suffering of animals that have no moral responsibility?
22. Is it logical to suppose that people are perfectly happy in their first human incarnation, before having any karma?
23. Does the doctrine of karma inspire the hope of soon being free from suffering?
24. What does karma really embrace?
25. What factors determine man's condition in life when born into human form?

Chapter 8, **Facts and Fancies About Reincarnation - 2**

1. Why is it easy to mistake a psychometric rapport with an astral record as an experience in a past life?
2. How are the real experiences of the soul during sleep often mistaken for an experience in a past life?
3. Why is genius no proof of past incarnation in human form?
4. What determined the first human incarnation?
5. What is the Cycle of Naros?
6. Why do certain types of people periodically recur?
7. What is the Anthem of Creative Life?
8. Is stagnation part of Nature's plan? Why?
9. Are Nature's limits so narrow she must force man back upon earth to relearn the lessons he has already been taught?
10. Why do people who recall past lives remember they were some notable person?
11. Why is human reincarnation not strictly an occult doctrine?
12. Why is it taught that the Dalai Lama is a reincarnation of Buddha?

13. In what way does the doctrine of human reincarnation tend to make the masses willing slaves of kings and potentates?
14. What teaching of Moslemism has for its purpose the subjugation of the masses?
15. What Christian teaching appeals to the selfish instincts of man and tends to keep him from rising against oppression?
16. Why has the priesthood always opposed the advance of science?
17. Why is the Caste System the natural outgrowth of the doctrine of human reincarnation?
18. Why is human reincarnation the most successful dogma ever taught for keeping the masses contented with their lot?
19. Do ideas reincarnate?
20. What are the exceptional cases in which there is human reincarnation?
21. What part has karma to play in life after death?
22. Why do Eastern priests discourage investigation of the spiritual realm?
23. What is the teaching the world needs at present?
24. Why have the people of the West made greater strides in civilization than those of the East?
25. Why is the teaching of human reincarnation destructive?

Chapter 9, The Ritual of Egyptian Initiation

1. From whence were the elaborate ceremonies of the Samothracian Mysteries, Eleusis, Bacchus, and the Saturnalia, derived?
2. Who was Iamblichus, and what did he write?
3. What does "Riding the Goat" symbolize?
4. What were the objectives of the trials during initiation?
5. What are the sex doctrines of the ancient Mysteries?
6. In what scriptural allegory is the separation of the ego into male and female souls described?
7. What does the murder and reconstruction of Osiris symbolically picture?
8. What does the whole ritual symbolize?
9. What does the candidate's journey to the foot of the sphinx represent?
10. What does the sphinx symbolize?
11. What does the descending spiral stairway of 22 steps symbolize?
12. What is signified by the arms of the candidate crossed on his

breast?

13. What does the abyss upon the edge of which the neophyte is halted represent?
14. What does the mechanical spectre swinging the scythe at the neophyte's neck seven times indicate?
15. What does the first dark tunnel symbolize, and what does the inverted cone with a well at the bottom represent?
16. What does climbing up 7 steps of the iron ladder and passing through the cleft in the rocks represent?
17. What does the door of bronze symbolize?
18. What does a golden rose symbolize?
19. What is signified by the 7 lamps of 3 branches each?
20. What is indicated by the Hierophant wearing a band of gold about his brow and occupying a throne of silver?
21. What does the triangle from which flow the golden rays, and the equilateral triangle of silver meeting at the top of the forehead of Isis, symbolize?
22. What does the second oath represent?
23. What does the royal nuptial chamber symbolize?
24. What does the garland of flowers indicate?
25. What is symbolized by the sphinx destroying the human effigy?

Appendix _____

The following natal charts are reprinted here for the use and interest of the student of astrology. The brief biographical sketches are provided to illustrate astrological correspondences to significant life events. The horoscopes of notable personalities were chosen because some aspects of their lives and character are already familiar to the public, and can more easily be correlated with the astrological factors shown.

Permission to freely use and reproduce these charts is hereby granted by the Church of Light.

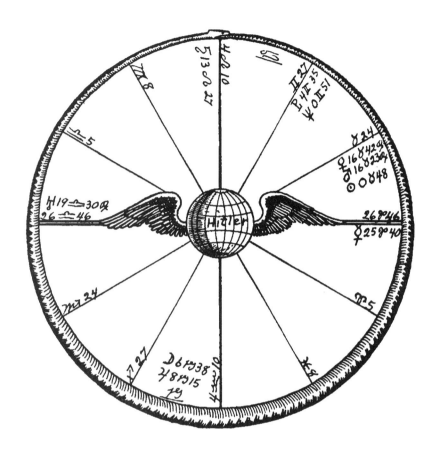

Adolph Hitler, April 20, 1889, 6:30 p.m. L.M.T. 13E 48N.

    1914,   lance corporal in World War: Mars (ruler of house of war)
            sesqui-square Uranus r.

    1919,   became obsessed with idea of regenerating Germany: Sun con-
            junction Neptune r (planet of big schemes and of ideals).

    1923,   with Ludendorf, attempted putsch in Bavaria failed, and he
            was imprisoned: Sun sesqui-square Uranus p in house of im-
            prisonment.

    1931,   civil war: Mars semi-square Sun r in house of war.

    1933,   became dictator of Germany: Sun sextile Saturn r in 10th
            (house of honor).

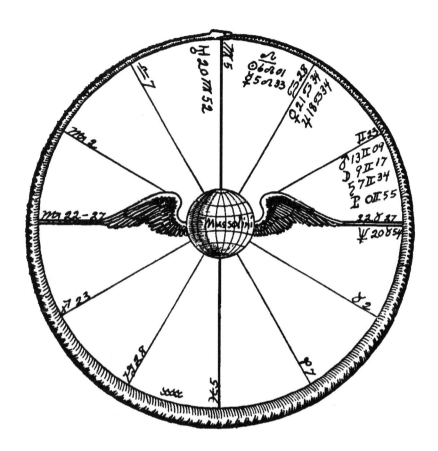

Benito Mussolini, July 29, 1883, 2:00 p.m. LMT 16 E 41 N.

    1914, expelled from socialist ranks for advocating war: Sun conjunction M.C. r (honor); Mercury trine Pluto r in house of war.

    1919, March 23, first Fascisti meeting: Sun in 10th (honor) square Saturn r; Venus conjunction M.C. r (honor) sextile Mars p.

    1922, October 30, March on Rome, became dictator of Italy: Sun in 10th square Mars r in house of war; Mercury trine Moon r (people).

    1935, October, war with Ethiopia: Venus conjunction Sun p in 10th; Mercury square Venus r; Mars semi-square Pluto r in house of war.

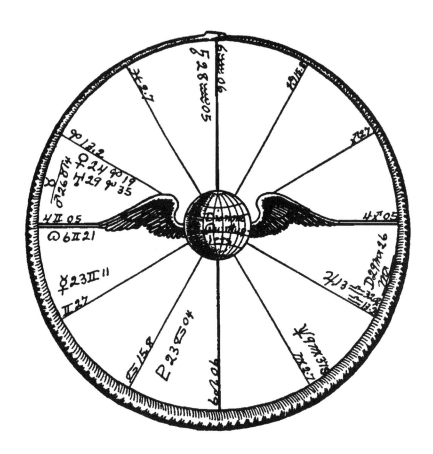

Dionne Quintuplets, May 28, 1934, 4:30 a.m. EST   79 W 15   46 N 15.

The first was born a few minutes after 4:00 a.m., and Dr. Dafoe states Yvonne, Annette, Cecile, Emilie and Marie all were born by 5:00 a.m. First Quintuplets ever known to have lived an hour (Sun conjunction Asc. is strongest possible position for vitality). Béing members of a group is indicated by Pluto in the house of brethren (third). The Doctor has it in the house of fame (tenth) and there was a progressed aspect from the planet of abundance (Jupiter), ruler of children (fifth), to it. He has Sun in sign of multiple births (Gemini) and they have both Sun and Ascendant there.

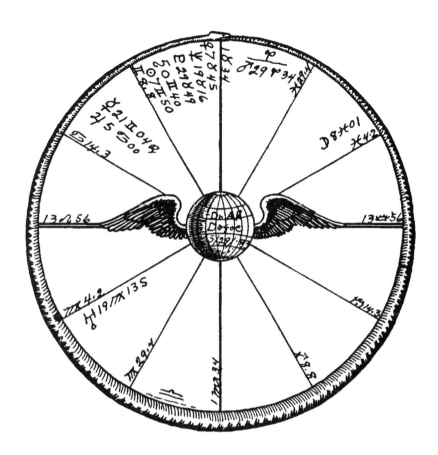

Dr. Allan Roy Dafoe, May 29, 1883, 9:30 a.m. LMT 77 W 30 44 N 20.

> **1887,** accident leaving deep scars on head, and causing him to stammer from that time on: Mercury square Uranus r.
>
> **1908,** license to practice, diphtheria epidemic, saved lives of many people through antitoxin, lost job because company objected to its expense: Venus conjunction Sun r, and square Moon r.
>
> **1918-19,** saved many lives in flu epidemic: Mercury square Uranus p, Venus conjunction Mercury p, Sun conjunction Jupiter p.
>
> **1931,** gained lasting fame in delivery of Dionne Quintuplets, Government made him their medical guardian: Mars conjunction Saturn r, Jupiter semi-square Pluto t, Mercury semi-square Pluto r.

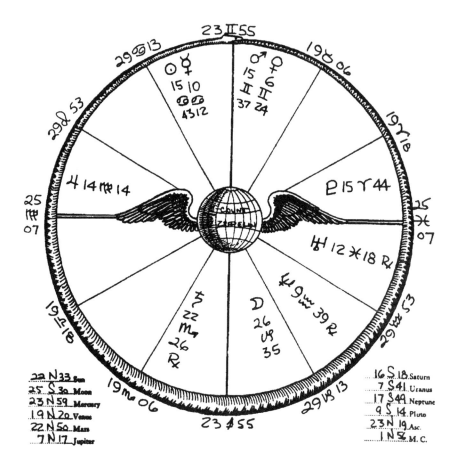

Count Zeppelin, July 8, 1838, 10:30 a.m. 9 E 20 47 N 38. Data German
astrological periodical.

1858, commission in army: Venus conjunction Mars p in M.C.

1862-3, volunteer under Grant in Civil War, first time balloon used
in any warfare: Sun opposition Neptune (aviation planet).

1890, started to build first airship: Venus opposition Neptune p.

1900, first airship flight, in air 20 minutes, wrecked in landing: Mars
sextile Jupiter p, Mars opposition Moon r.

1906, successful airship flight, speed 30 miles per hour: Jupiter trine
Moon r, Venus semi-sextile Jupiter r.

1913, first dirigible regular sea service: Sun trine Moon r.

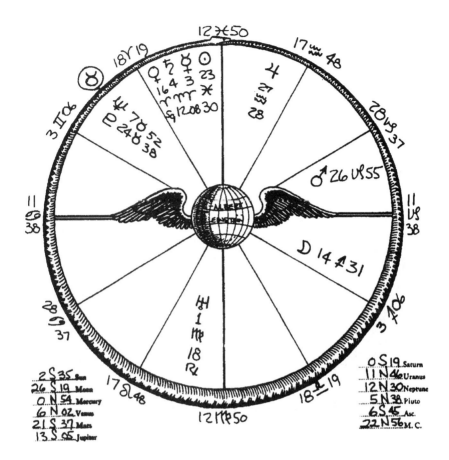

Albert Einstein, March 14, 1879, 11:30 a.m. 10 E 48 N 24. Data, *Practical Astrology,* February, 1930.

1900, examiner of patents at Berne: Sun trine Moon r.

1905, published Restricted Theory of Relativity: Mercury trine Uranus r.

1915, published General Theory of Relativity: Sun trine Uranus p. 1921, member Royal Society: Sun semi-sextile Saturn r.

1933, professor of mathematics at Princeton: Mercury sextile Venus p. 1939, announced mathematical bridge embracing gravitational field electromagnetic field and material particles: Mercury square Mars r Venus sextile Uranus p.

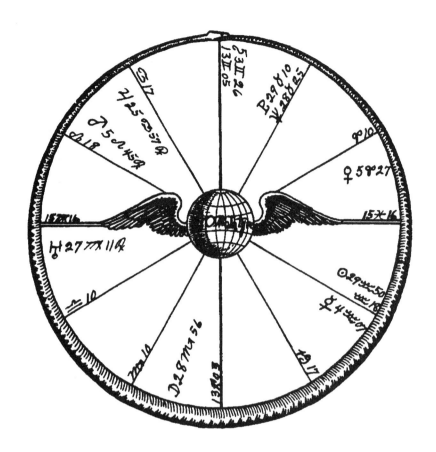

O. O. McIntyre, February 18, 1884, 6:53 p.m. LMT 94 W 30 39 N 30.
  1903, after futile nine months at business college, invested all his
       cash in 9 telegrams to newspapers asking for job; one hired
       him: Mercury in conjunct Mars p, Sun sextile Neptune r.
  1904, made city editor, then managing editor: Venus in conjunct
       Moon;, Venus semi-sextile Pluto r, Mercury in conjunct Mars p.
  1911, induced by Ray Long to go to New York for magazine work,
       was literary high-light for brief period, then sank to mere
       press agent: Sun opposition Uranus p.
  After this set-back started to climb. His column "New York Day by
       Day," has appeared daily for 20 years, and at the moment this
       is written (1937) he is said to be the highest paid journalist in

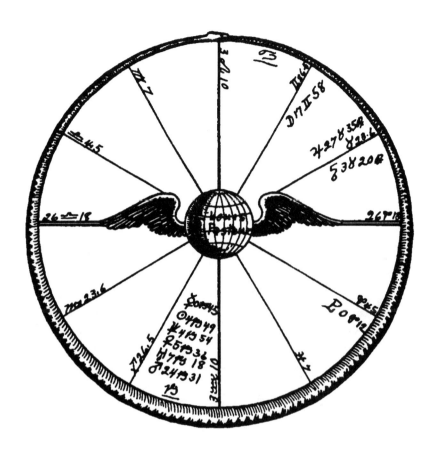

Louis Pasteur, December 27, 1822, 2:02 a.m. 5 E 30 47N.

    1848, became professor at university: Sun sextile Pluto r.

    1854, became dean of scientific faculty: Sun semi-sextile Uranus r
        Mercury semi-square Uranus r Mars trine Moon r.

    1865, studied and solved silkworm disease: Sun trine Moon r.

    1866, decided infection due to microbes: Venus semi-sextile Pluto r
        Venus sextile Mercury r Mercury sextile Venus r.

    1885, discovered anti-toxin: Sun sextile Uranus r, Mercury semi-
        square Uranus r.

    1889, withdrew from all other pursuits to manage Pasteur Institute:
        Venus trine Uranus r Sun semi-sextile Jupiter r, Mars square
        Uranus p.

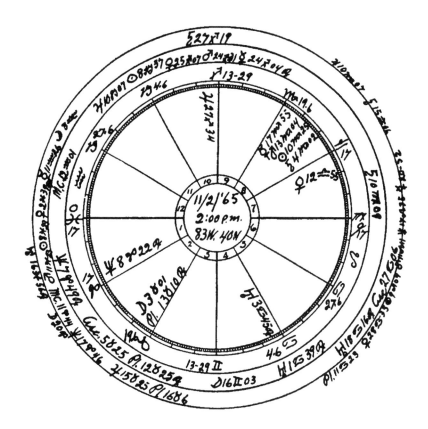

Warren G. Harding, Nov. 2, 1865, 2:00 p.m. 83 W 40 N. Major Progressions, Minor Progressions, and Transits outside the chart, all for Aug. 2, 1923.

  1910, unsuccessful candidate for governor of Ohio: Sun semi-square Sun r, Mercury conjunction Jupiter p.

  1920, elected president of US: Mercury conjunction Jupiter r, Venus conjunction Mars p in 10th.

  1923, August 2, died of ptomaine poisoning: Sun square Neptune r. Minor Sun semi-sextile Neptune r, sextile Sun p. Transit Sun trine Neptune r.

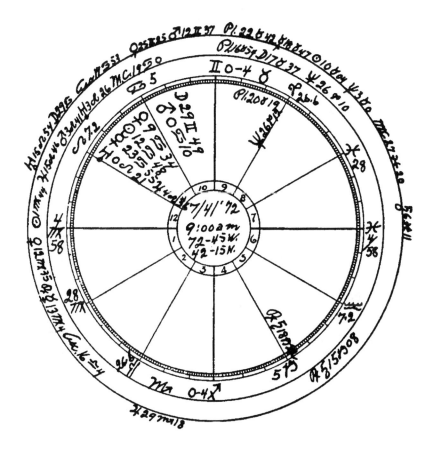

Calvin Coolidge, July 4, 1872, 9:00 a.m. 72 W 45 42 N 15. Major
Progressions in outer circle are for Aug. 3, 1923. Minor Progressions
on outside of chart are for Aug. 3, 1923.

1897, began practice of law: Mars, co-ruler of 10th, opposition
Saturn p.

1905, married: Mercury sesqui-square Neptune, ruler of 7th.

1923, became President of U. S. through death of Harding: As
progressed above, M.C. opposition Saturn r, Mars conjunction
Uranus p, Asc. sextile Jupiter p, Mercury conjunction Venus p.
Minor Mars square Venus p and Mercury p, Uranus conjunction Jupiter p.

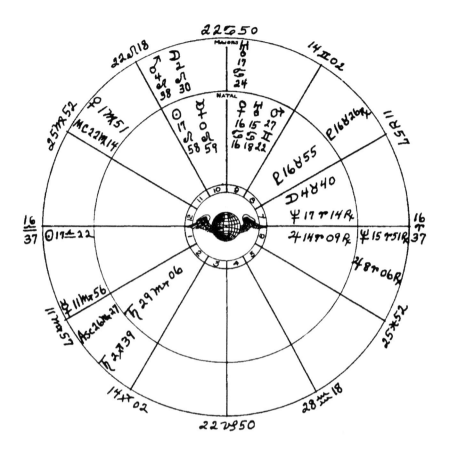

Captain Hugo Eckener, August 10, 1868 10:22 a.m. LMT Flensburg, Germany. 54 N 47 9 E 26. Major progressions in outer circle are for August, 1929.

  1928, October, first flight of lighter-than-air craft to America: Sun square Venus r, Sun conjunction Asc. r.

  1929, August, first round-the-world flight in lighter-than-air craft: Sun opposition Neptune r, Sun square Uranus p, Mars square, Moon r.

  1931, July, arctic cruise in Graf Zeppelin: Venus trine Moon r, Mercury in conjunct Jupiter r.

  1934, October, proposed commercial air service between Germany and America; proposal accepted: Mercury trine Uranus p,

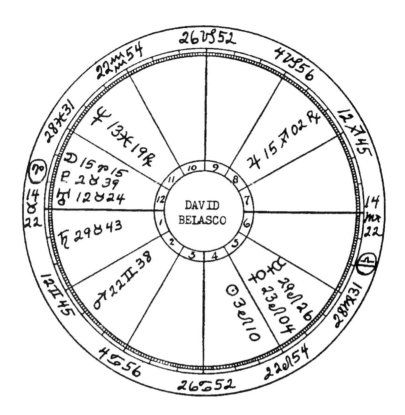

David Belasco, July 25, 1853, 11:40 p.m. LMT San Francisco, Calif. 37 N 47 122 W 26.

Famous (ruler of 10th in 1st, trine M.C.) theatrical producer: Venus conjunction Mercury in 5th, house of the theatre, forming a Grand Trine to Moon in 12th and Jupiter in 8th.

Abundant money from public: Jupiter in 8th, forming Grand Trine to Moon in 12th and Venus in 5th.

Dramatic ability: Neptune elevated, sextile Asc., semi-sextile Moon.

Originality: Uranus conjunction the Asc.

Co-operation with others: Pluto square Sun, trine Mercury.

Organization, system, perseverance: Saturn in 1st, sextile Sun.

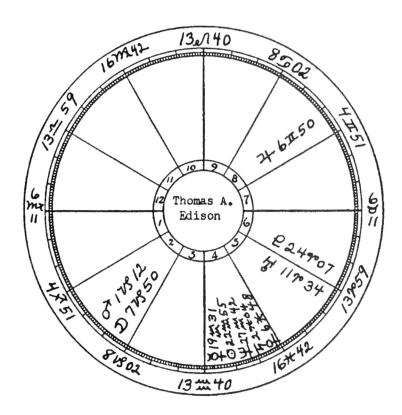

Thomas A. Edison, February 11, 1847, 11:38 p.m. LMT Milan, Ohio
41 N 18   82 W 37.

World's greatest inventor (Uranus square Moon and Mars), and
world's greatest expert on source and use of materials (Sun, Mercury
and Neptune conjunction Saturn in 4th).

Lost money in companies promoting his inventions (Uranus in 5th,
square Mars in 2nd).

Was endowed (Jupiter in 8th, sextile Uranus) in such a way that if
he lost his own money he could continue his experiments.

Fame through inventions (Uranus trine M. C.).

Had loyal support of employees, and contributed immensely to
human welfare (Pluto, universal welfare planet, in 6th, sextile Sun,

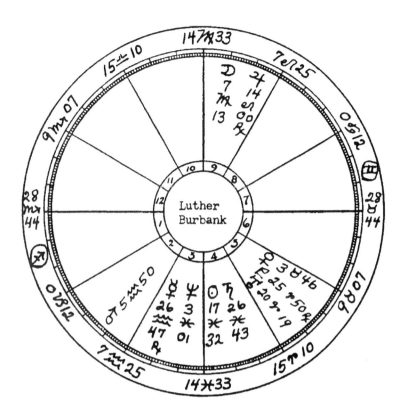

Luther Burbank, March 7, 1849, 11:59:60 p.m. LMT Lancaster, Mass.
42 N 27 71W41.

Fame as world's greatest plant breeder and horticulturist (Sun in 4th, opposition M. C., conjunction Saturn, semi-sextile Uranus).

Developed innumerable varieties of useful vegetables, fruits and flowers through chance (Pluto and Uranus in 5th, sextile Mercury) variations Efforts contributed greatly to human welfare (Pluto, universal welfare planet, semi-sextile Saturn, conjunction Uranus, sextile Mercury)

At an advanced age orthodox churches attacked him as an unbeliever (Jupiter in 9th opposition Mars), and the bitter controversy in which he engaged is believed to hastened his death (Sun in house ruling

Index

Other Brotherhood of Light Books _____

_____

The following pages present brief descriptions of the 21 Brotherhood of Light courses, written by C. C. Zain. The information contained therein represents the ancient wisdom of the Hermetic Tradition, transmitted orally in earlier ages only to initiates of The Brotherhood of Light. It was the life's work of Elbert Benjamine, under the pen name of C. C. Zain, to present this complete system of esoteric knowledge in an organized format, available for the first time to the public.

CS. 1, Laws of Occultism

Inner Plane Theory and the Fundamentals of Psychic Phenomena

$14.95   6x9   192pp

The word "occult" means hidden or unseen. *The Laws of Occultism* is the study of unseen energies and the subjugation of these energies, insofar as we are able, to human control. There are in existence undeviating natural laws that are yet unexplained by physical science. In this course various types of psychic phenomena are examined and explained. The nature of the inner plane and how it affects human life and activities is revealed.

1. Occult Data **2.** Astral Substance **3.** Astral Vibrations **4.** Doctrine of Nativities **5.** Doctrine of Mediumship **6.** Spiritism **7.** Phenomenal Spiritism

---

CS. 2, Astrological Signatures

Evolution and the Soul and the Nature of Astrological Energies

$14.95   6x9   256pp

This is our best book for those beginning their study of astrology. The Signs of the Zodiac, the Planets, the Mundane Houses and the Aspects are all discussed in detail. The philosophy of "The Religion of the Stars" concerning the nature of the soul, how it makes progress and why the experiences of life are necessary to prepare it for a higher destiny is presented. Of special interest are the chapters concerning the facts and fancies of reincarnation and the ancient ritual of Egyptian Initiation.

1. The Two Keys **2.** The Zodiac **3.** Mundane Houses **4.** The Mission of the Soul **5.** Physiology and Correspondence **6.** Doctrine of Signatures **7.** Facts and Fancies About Reincarnation I **8.** Facts and Fancies About Reincarnation II **9.** The Ritual of Egyptian Initiation

---

CS. 3, Spiritual Alchemy

The Hermetic Art of Spiritual Transformation

$14.95   6x9   128pp

The ancient alchemist sought transmutation and immortality. For the soul to be immortal it must build for itself an imperishable spiritual body in which it can function after the dissolution of both the physical and astral forms. The experiences of life are symbolized by the metals of alchemy. Through proper mental attitude we purify the metals, develop our character and create our destiny. The various states of consciousness available to man are set forth and analyzed.

1. Doctrine of Spiritual Alchemy **2.** Seven Spiritual Metals **3.** Purifying the Metals **4.** Transmutation **5.** Higher Consciousness

CS. 4, Ancient Masonry

The Spiritual Meaning of Masonic Degrees, Rituals and Symbols

$14.95   6x9   336pp

In this course the rituals and symbols of Ancient Masonry are revealed. For the modern Freemason this is an unprecedented work enabling him to perceive the esoteric and spiritual significance of the symbols and all things done in the lodge room. The astrological significance of the symbols and their relationship to soul-development are thoroughly discussed.

1. Ancient Masonry Introduction **2.** Entered Apprentice and the Planets **3.** Entered Apprentice and the Signs **4.** Numbers and Opening the Lodge **5.** Initiating a Member **6.** Fellowcraft **7.** Lodge Emblems **8.** Master Mason **9.** Mark Master Mason **10.** Royal Arch **11.** Degrees of the Cross **12.** Ineffable Degrees **13.** Historical Degrees

---

CS. 5, Esoteric Psychology

Success Through Directed Thinking and Induced Emotion

$14.95   6x9   320pp

Of all the energies that influence man none have a more powerful effect than his own thoughts. Directing one's thinking is the most potent of all forces to control one's life and destiny. Commonly, our efforts to exercise control are hindered due to faulty conceptions or repressions that result from environmental conditioning. Whether this conditioning expresses in a subtle way or in one that is more obvious, the consequence is a thwart to progress. Esoteric Psychology contains information which will assist in identifying and eliminating these obstacles to progress.

1. Doctrine of Esoteric Psychology **2.** Reason and Intuition **3.** Language and the Value of Dreams **4.** Desire and How to Use It **5.** Why Repression is Not Morality **6.** How to Rule the Stars **7.** How to Apply Suggestion **8.** Correct Use of Affirmations **9.** How to Think Constructively **10.** How to Cultivate Subliminal Thinking **11.** How to Develop Creative Imagination **12.** How to Demonstrate Success

---

CS. 6, Sacred Tarot

The Art of Card Reading and the Underlying Spiritual Science

$14.95   6x9   336pp

The Sacred Tarot is a favorite of metaphysical students everywhere and companion to the *Brotherhood of Light Egyptian Tarot Cards*. With this book, the student can readily determine the astrological correspondence of any number, name, color, gem or other object. In this course the "Religion of the Stars" system of numerology is set forth and divination by means of numbers is explained. It is also considered to be one of the most complete, detailed syntheses of the Tarot archetypes as they manifest spiritual truths in different areas of occult science. Each of the 78 cards is explained and 11 tarot card spreads are illustrated.

1. Doctrine of Kabalism **2.** Foundation of the Science **3.** Scope and Use of Tarot **4.** Involution and Evolution of Numbers **5.** Reading the Meaning of Numbers **6.** Making an Astrological Chart of a Name **7.** Influence of Changing the Name **8.** Reading Names in Detail **9.** The Color of a Name **10.** Natural Talismans and Artificial Charms **11.** Chronology of the Tarot **12.** Solution of Ancient Cycles **13.** How to Read the Tarot

CS. 7, Spiritual Astrology

The Origins of Astro-Mythology and Stellar Religion

$14.95   6x9   352pp

This course describes the outstanding attributes of those born under the influence of each of the 48 ancient constellations. Also revealed are the specific spiritual doctrines associated with each of the constellations. These spiritual doctrines, formulated by the most wise of prehistoric times, later found their way into ancient mythology, the Bible and other sacred writings. Course VII sets forth the most significant of these stories associated with these doctrines and reveals their true meaning.

1. Our Spiritual Legacy 2. The Fountain of Youth 3. Knights of King Arthur 4. Story of the Three Bears 5. The Ladder to Heaven 6. Is There a Santa Claus 7. Why Eve Was Tempted 8. The Marriage in Heaven 9. The Scorpion and the Eagle 10. The Bow of Bright Promise 11. News From the Summerland 12. In the Reign of Aquarius 13. The Tree of Life

---

CS. 8, Horary Astrology

How to Erect and Judge a Horoscope

$14.95   6x9   224pp

This course is often chosen by beginning students of astrology for its technical lesson, "How to Erect a Horoscope", as well as for its clearly organized system for judging any horoscope. More advanced students refer to this volume for horary chart interpretation. The section on horary astrology is of special interest for its explanation of how and why this branch of astrology can solve a problem relating to events past, present and future. Also included for beginning students are CCZain's chart erection short-cuts, for which he designed the Church of Light #2 Chartpad.

1. How to Erect a Horoscope 2. Strength and Aspects of the Planets 3. First Seven Steps in Judging Any Horoscope 4. The Doctrine of Horary Astrology 5. Questions Relating to First Six Houses 6. Questions Relating to Last Six Houses 7. How to Select the Best Time for any Undertaking 8. Chart Erection Short Cuts and Examples

---

CS. 9, Mental Alchemy

How Thoughts and Feelings Shape Our Lives

$14.95   6x9   224pp

The astrological energies mapped by a birthchart are not the cause of the conditions and events that come into one's life. It is the character of the individual that determines our destiny. Character is composed of thought cells built and organized on the inner plane. Course IX explains how these thought cell groups, which constitute man's unconscious mind, have been formed before his birth, and how they are modified after birth by experience. Of importance is an explanation of how these thought cells can and should be reconditioned to work for the things the individual desires.

1. The Inner Nature of Poverty, Failure and Disease 2. Just How to Find the Thought-Cause of Any Condition 3. How to Find a Mental Antidote 4. How to Apply a Mental Antidote 5. Just How to Heal Yourself 6. Just How to Attain Realization 7. Just How to Give Absent Treatments

CS. 10-1, Natal Astrology, Part One

Delineating the Horoscope

$14.95   6x9   224pp

As the Lessons on astrology emphasize, much is to be gained through a diligent application of the rules when interpreting a horoscope. In a step-by-step fashion, Delineating the Horoscope presents the Hermetic system of natal astrology along with the unsurpassed "Outline of a Complete Astrological Reading." Beginning and advanced students will enjoy the explanations of the 36 decanates, illustrated with examples of renowned persons having Sun, Moon or Ascendant in that decanate.

1. First Eighteen Decanates Analyzed **2.** Last Eighteen Decanates Analyzed **3.** Stature, Temperament, Disposition and Mental Ability **4.** Vitality, Health and Disease **5.** Business, Finances and Vocational Selection **6.** Friends, Enemies and Associates **7.** Love, Marriage and Partnership **8.** How to Delineate a Horoscope

CS. 10-2, Natal Astrology, Part Two

Progressing the Horoscope

$14.95   6x9   224pp

A technical manual on the Hermetic system of major and minor progressions. The progressed aspects of natal astrology reveal probable future events through indicating the manner in which an individual's thought-cells will work to attract events. With this information the individual can learn to take precautionary actions by reconditioning the energy so that a more desirable outcome can be achieved. To round out the study of natal astrology, a lesson on the Hermetic system of rectifying the horoscope is included for use in erecting a birthchart when the exact birth time is unknown.

1. Hermetic System of Progressions **2.** Major Progressions of Sun and Angles **3.** Major Progressions of the Moon **4.** Major Progressions of the Planets **5.** Minor Progressions of the Sun and Angles **6.** Minor Progressions of the Moon and Planets **7.** Transits, Revolutions and Cycles **8.** Rectifying the Horoscope

CS. 11, Divination & Character Reading

Tools and Techniques for Enhancing ESP

$14.95   6x9   192pp

Divination is a means for assisting extension of consciousness on the inner plane to acquire the information desired. It is then brought up into the region of objective consciousness. Clairvoyance, precognition, telepathy, the divining rod, teacup and coffee cup methods, among others, are discussed in detail. The last four lessons are devoted to learning to read character based on physical characteristics.

1. Doctrine of Divination **2.** Tea-cup and Coffee-cup Divination **3.** Divining Rod and Other Divination **4.** Instantaneous Character Reading **5.** Significance of Body and Head **6.** Instantaneous Reading from Profile **7.** Instantaneous Vocational Analysis

CS. 12-1, Natural Alchemy, Part One

Evolution of Life

$14.95   6x9   224pp

We live in kinship with all life forms, animate and inanimate. For man to understand his place in nature, and thus what his relation should be to other life-forms, to other people, and to God, he needs to know how the various life-forms, including man, have developed to the state they now occupy. Cs. XII-1 offers the unique interpretation of the Religion of the Stars on how natural selection and adaptation is influenced by psychokinesis, ESP and inner-plane influence.

1. Origin of the Earth **2.** Origin and Development of Plants **3.** Progress of Invertebrate Life **4.** Fishes and Amphibians **5.** Reptiles and Birds **6.** Development Among Mammals **7.** Development of Man **8.** Development of Knowledge

---

CS. 12-2, Natural Alchemy, Part Two

Evolution of Religion

$14.95   6x9   224pp

This course deals with the evolution of those ideas which constitute man's various religions. Cs. XII-2 begins with the most primitive religions and shows how these, and the cultures coincident with them, gradually developed into the more complex systems of belief of today. The tenets of each important present day religion are explained, and finally there is set forth the basic tenets of the Religion of the Stars.

1. The Foundations of Religion **2.** Early Religions of the World **3.** Religion in Historic Times **4.** Tao, Confucianism, Zoroastrianism and Mohammedanism **5.** Hinduism and Buddhism **6.** Judaism and Christianity **7.** The Stellarian Religion **8.** Astrology is Religion's Road Map

---

CS. 13, Mundane Astrology

Interpreting Astrological Phenomena for Cities, Nations and Groups

$14.95   5X7   272pp

Astrological energies influence the trend of world events. When a natal chart isn't available, these influences can be determined through the mundane cycle charts of nations, cities, groups, etc. This course is one of the few technical manuals on the erection of mundane cycle charts and their delineation. Such information is valuable because it enables one to take precautionary actions and arrange personal affairs to take most advantage of city, national or world conditions. It also helps one to foresee conditions and thus exert political influence in support of those measures which insure peace and give people freedom from want, freedom from fear, freedom of expression and freedom of religion.

1. Doctrine of Mundane Astrology **2.** Cycles of Pluto and Neptune **3.** Cycles of Uranus **4.** Cycles of Saturn **5.** Cycles of Jupiter **6.** Cycles of Mars **7.** Major Conjunctions of the Planets **8.** Cycles of the Sun **9.** Cycles of the Moon **10.** Precise Predicting:Eclipses

CS. 14, Occultism Applied

How to Increase Your Happiness, Usefulness and Spirituality

$14.95   6x9   320pp

Just how to use occult knowledge and occult energies in everyday life is considered in detail in Course XIV. It shows us that each soul is being trained for its own cosmic work and has its own kind of job to do in God's Great Evolutionary Plan, pointing out the advantage of living the completely constructive life. To gain the things we desire from life usually requires that some of our habit systems be changed. Changing habits is not easy, but the three fundamental principles given in Cs. XIV will give the quickest and surest success.

1. Finding One's Cosmic Work **2.** Living the Completely Constructive Life **3.** Diet and Breathing **4.** How to Keep Young **5.** How to Be Attractive **6.** How to Have Friends **7.** How to Get Employment **8.** How to Make Money **9.** How to Achieve Honors **10.** How to Be Successful in Marriage **11.** How to Have a Pleasant Home **12.** How to Be Happy

---

CS. 15, Weather Predicting

The Hermetic System of Astrological Weather Analysis

$14.95   6x9   192pp

Astrological energies have a profound influence over the weather conditions of earth. They indicate changes from the normal of a given locality in temperature, moisture and wind, quite precisely. This is particularly useful information for those involved in agriculture, aviation, travel or planning a social event. It is an aspect of the science that should not be neglected by anyone seeking a complete, working knowledge of astrology. *Weather Predicting* is a complete treatment of the subject and the only text available entirely devoted to astrological influences on the weather.

1. Astrological Weather Predicting **2.** Reading Astrological Weather Charts **3.** Astrological Temperature Charts **4.** Astrological Air Movement Charts **5.** Astrological Moisture Charts **6.** Unusual Weather **7.** Tornadoes and Hurricanes

---

CS. 16, Stellar Healing

Astrological Predisposition, Diagnosis and Treatment of Disease

$14.95   6x9   320pp

Health is a valuable asset. The positions of the planets in the birthchart indicate the diseases toward which an individual is predisposed. *Stellar Healing* gives the birthchart and progressed constants of 160 diseases. It also sets forth what is probably the most effective of all methods of drugless healing, and indicates the specific Stellar Treatment. In addition, it shows how to calculate in terms of ASTRODYNES, HARMODYNES and DISCORDYNES the precise power and harmony of any planet, aspect, sign or house. ASTRODYNES are the unsurpassed mathematical formula for the measurement of astrological power.

1. Stellar Anatomy **2.** Basis of Stellar Diagnosis **3.** Principles of Stellar Healing **4.** Technique of Stellar Healing **5.** Stellar Healing in Practice **6.** Diagnosis and Treatment **7.** Abdominal Troubles -Bleeding **8.** Blindness -Coronary Thrombosis **9.** Cyst -Hay Fever **10.** Headache -Mumps **11.** Nervous Breakdown -Scarlet Fever **12.** Sciatica- Yellow Fever

CS. 17, Cosmic Alchemy

The Spiritual Guide to Universal Progression

$14.95   6x9   256pp

Man is not an isolated unit. Instead he is a member of world society, and should be an energetic worker in the realization of God's Great Evolutionary Plan. This course indicates how each person can become active in achieving the realization of this plan. In this progress there will be no more wars, poverty will be abolished, educational facilities and the widest access to information should be available to all. Cs. XVII shows exactly what spirituality is and the three general methods of gaining it; 1. viewing events from the standpoint of spiritual alchemy, 2. cultivating thoughts, feelings and actions that arise from the desire to benefit others, and 3. raising the vibratory rate through a heightened intellectual and emotional appreciation.

1. Conquest of War **2.** Abolition of Poverty **3.** Cosmic Politics **4.** Heredity and Environment **5.** How to Be Spiritual **6.** Spiritual Value of Education **7.** How to Appraise Spiritual Values **8.** Minor Aids to Spiritual Advancements **9.** Major Aids to Spiritual Advancements

---

CS. 18, Imponderable Forces

The Wholesome Pathway

$14.95   6x9   192pp

Cs. XVIII explains how much reliance should be placed on transits, minor progressed aspects, major progressed aspects and other astrological conditions, and the proper attitude toward such astrological weather. It indicates how sympathies and antipathies work and how much importance to attribute to birthstones, numbers, names and environmental vibrations. Since the greatest enemy of fear and superstition is thorough understanding, this course explains in detail ceremonial magic, sorcery and witchcraft, and how to protect oneself against black magic of any kind. It shows how to avoid the influence of suggestion and inversive propaganda. *Imponderable Forces* gives a comprehensive survey of the wholesome pathway, and how to follow it.

1. How to Act Under Adverse Progressed Aspects **2.** Sympathies and Antipathies **3.** Ceremonial Magic **4.** Sorcery and Witchcraft **5.** Ritual and Religion **6.** Press, Radio and Billboard **7.** The Wholesome Pathway.

CS. 19, Organic Alchemy

The Universal Law of Soul Progression

$14.95   6x9   192pp

To live in harmony with nature's laws we must understand them. Humans are not set apart from other living things, but all life forms come under one uniform, universal law. This course explains how soul progress occurs; its original polarity, as indicated by its astrological signature, is energized by its ego and conditioned through pleasure and pain. Nature uses pleasure and pain, not as reward or punishment, but to inform the organism whether is it successfully adapting to its environment. Cs. XIX gives information about the problems and habits of other life forms, why there is no unpardonable sin, how the cosmos is managed and an outline of the general cosmic plan.

1. The Ceaseless Surge of Life **2.** Every Life Form Manifests a Soul **3.** The Universal Law of Soul Progression **4.** The Uses of Pleasure and Pain **5.** The Universal Law of Compensation **6.** The Universal Moral Code **7.** Discerning God's Great Plan

CS. 20, The Next Life

A Guide to Living Conditions on the Inner Plane

$14.95   6x9   272pp

Life on earth is but one phase of existence. Physical life constitutes necessary schooling so that the soul can function effectively on a higher plane where it will be less restricted. By understanding the nature of the life to come, the individual is better prepared to live this life and the next. Course XX gives a great deal of information about the conditions to be met and the activities of life after physical death. It tells about the various levels of the inner plane world, about the three methods of birth into the next life, about the influence of desires there, of the effect of sorrowing for those who have passed to the next life and how they may be helped, of the work to be done there and how education is handled. *The Next Life* is not only interesting, but the information it contains will be a highly valuable guide to anyone when they pass from the physical.

1. Turning the Dial to Inner Planes **2.** Properties of Life on The Inner Plane **3.** Birth Into the Next Life **4.** Astrological Influences in the Next Life **5.** Occupations of the Next Life **6.** Education and Progress in the Next Life **7.** Earth Bound Souls and the Astral Hells **8.** Domestic Relations of the Next Life **9.** Social Contacts and Amusements in the Next Life **10.** Through Astral and Spiritual to Celestial

---

CS. 21, Personal Alchemy

The Neophyte's Path to Spiritual Attainment

$14.95   6x9   272pp

The student who has gained the knowledge contained in the first 20 Brotherhood of Light courses is apt to decide to develop himself and his powers to the very best advantage. Consequently, *Personal Alchemy* gives precise instructions on the steps such an individual should take, and the order in which he should take them.

1. Three Things Every Neophyte Should Know **2.** The First Three Habits a Neophyte Should Adopt **3.** Avenues to Illumination **4.** Spiritual Hindrance by Family and Friends **5.** Spiritual Trends in Personal Conduct **6.** How to Keep Mentally and Physically Fit **7.** What to Eat When Mercury or Uranus is Afflicted **8.** What to Eat When Sun, Moon or Pluto is Afflicted **9.** What to Eat When Saturn, Jupiter or Neptune is Afflicted **10.** What to Eat When Venus or Mars is Afflicted.

To Order Brotherhood of Light Books:

Qty	#	Item	Price	Amt

Please include shipping & handling charges:
$3.00 first item, $.50 for each additional item.

Subtotal	
Shipping	
TOTAL	

YES ! Please send me a free catalog.

Ship To: _____

Address _____

City_____

State & Zip Code _____

Telephone _____

For ☐ **MasterCard** ☐ **Visa** Orders Only:

Card No. _____ **Exp Date** _____

Card Holder Signature _____

Send your check or money order to:

90031-2916

The Church of Light
111 S. Kraemer Blvd., Suite A
Brea, CA 92821